REAL MAN

This re-release of Dr. Edwin Louis Cole's classic best-seller,
Real Man, *was made possible in part by:*

Faithful Men Ministries
P. O. Box 612241
Dallas, TX 75261
www.fm318.com

watercolor books®

Southlake, Texas

Cover design by Mick Thurber

Second Edition
Real Man
ISBN 1-931682-12-7

CONTENTS

Part 1

The Masculinity Maze

1

The Masculinity Crisis

I LOVE BEING A MAN.

I don't feel ashamed, embarrassed, intimidated or guilty about it. But I know I'm not what I shall be. I am what I am, and I'm more than I was. But I'm not all the man I can be.

Today I know where I'm headed with my masculinity. For years I floundered in my attempts at manhood, never having been taught how to be a man. Through the struggles and difficulties, successes and rewards, I learned much of what being a man really means. Now I can say it's been a wonderful life in many ways. I have a wife I love deeply, children who have matured successfully, a career that—although erratic in some ways—is now a worldwide influence for good and God.

Many people recognize a current crisis in manhood and are trying to correct it. A headline in the *Boston Globe* read: "Wanted: Some Stouthearted Men." The article began with the question "What's wrong with America?" and gave this answer:

"Lousy leadership. Not just in government or politics, but in business and labor, service and manufacturing, education and other big institutions, and the media, too."[1]

Caustic and critical, but is it true? Most Americans would agree. We have a crisis in leadership and productivity—but this stems basically from a crisis in manhood. Our manhood has been emasculated, and that has sterilized our ability to reproduce.

The U.S. is not the only country suffering such problems. Scores of problems confront men in every nation under the sun. For example:

- South America's runaway inflation has sapped its countries' vitality, creating a fatalistic approach to life in its citizens. Young men feel they have nothing to look forward to and are helpless to do anything about the problem. Their crisis is not simply economic. It is a crisis in manhood.
- On my last visit to England, a major newspaper noted five million people were "on the dole." The article stated that the present generation of youth was without ambition or hope—they were gripped by a welfare mentality.
- Italian youth admire Mafia members more than government, religious or industry leaders, according to a recent report. Their next preference, after criminal celebrities, is entertainers. The reporter concluded that young people seem to lack any understanding of the normal values that undergird a productive society.
- When I was in Germany, its citizens said theirs is a "fatherless nation" because of the monumental loss of men in World War II.
- For the same reason, Russia is called a "nation without grandfathers." After World War II, only seventeen in a thousand Russians returned from battle, and only three of those seventeen were not wounded or maimed.[2]
- In Scotland, male depression runs rampant.
- In Australia and Central America, the "macho male" mentality has created problems in industry and family relationships.
- South African men still suffer from apartheid's aftermath.
- The Philippines endure a matriarchal society that has contributed to a high incidence of homosexuality among men.
- Reports of Nigerian men flagrantly brutalizing women have created a national concern and international embarrassment.

WHAT MAKES A MAN REAL?

People are motivated by what they *think* is important, whether or not that perception is true. The Bible puts it: "For as he thinks in his heart, so is he."[3] Perceptions of manhood, gleaned from society's role models—both good and bad—motivate men in behaviors that are both positive and negative. These society-dictated perceptions distort true manhood and create confusion. For example:

- Feminists rage against maleness, creating a new perception of the word *man*, and cry out to replace gender-specific terms with neuter terms.
- Gay-rights activists rage against heterosexuality and parade with "I hate straight" banners.
- Movies, television and entertainment give a perception of men as either stupid bunglers or super-macho heroes. Even "family" television programs show ineffective men depending on competent women to help them through life.
- Books and periodicals routinely criticize men for not spending enough time with the family, not doing their fair share of the work at home, not being sensitive to their wives ... and on the list goes.
- In the work place, other standards apply. Men are to behave aggressively—perfecting the art of the deal, making the sale, creating the new project, winning the contract, negotiating to the last penny. They are to compete through any available means—moral or otherwise.

Average men have tried to cope with these conflicting messages by trying to please everyone. They end up castrating their identity, becoming ineffective and sterile males. They hardly please anyone, instead becoming objects of displeasure. *No wonder men today are confused about manhood.*

In conferences and conventions, on radio and television programs, wherever I have ministered to men, one basic question consistently pops up: *What is a real man?*

Is a man to be like the actor, John Wayne, the swaggering, tough icon of old Hollywood's manliness—tall, strong, loyal to friends and a terror to enemies, always standing for right (always knowing what right is!), attractive to women, feared and respected by other men?

Or is a man to be like a talk-show host, television's answers to the feminist movement—sympathetic, emotional, sensitive, harmless? Or are men to revert to the idea of a "renaissance man"? Or are men to be like Nelson Mandela, Michael Jackson, Arnold Schwarzenegger or Nolan Ryan?

What is a real man? What is he like?

Answers spring from every sector—religion, philosophy, mythology, sociology, psychology, pop culture, education, government—everyone has an answer, but not every answer is true. Where, then, should we turn?

The answer to the masculinity crisis is the same answer given for every world crisis from the creation of time: the intervention of the Creator God. In the case of male identity and role, the answer is found in God as He revealed Himself on earth in the manhood of Jesus Christ.

Through Jesus, God showed us by example how to live as real men here on earth. God revealed to us in physical form what He had already said, that He created man in His image and for His purposes. Consequently *the essence of real manhood is found not in how a man looks or in what a man does but in who a man is.*

But this leads us to another problem that men have grappled with now for two thousand years. How do we approach this God-man, Jesus Christ? How could we even begin to emulate the deity of a holy God revealed on earth as a man? I admit I still don't have all the answers. But I *have* discovered numerous truths that I now teach around the world, and I *can* tell you that the results of applying these truths border on the incredible.

We have a crisis in leadership and productivity— but this stems basically from a crisis in manhood.

CHRISTLIKE MANHOOD

At one particular meeting, more than two thousand men crowded into an auditorium in Boston. Many of those attending would eventually take the patterns and principles I taught, embrace them, then teach other men, who in turn would teach others, and so the truth spreads. But on that day, as I spoke to those assembled, the revelation of Who Jesus really is and what He did for us as men seemed to pierce the minds and hearts of every man there. The weight of truth brought a quiet hush among them which, after several minutes, erupted into an enthusiastic expression of joy.

I stopped speaking to give an opportunity for the men who had never committed themselves to "real" manhood to come to the front and publicly make their stand. As hundreds came forward, the others spontaneously began to yell in unison, "Jesus, Jesus, Jesus!"

As they shouted, a conviction set in that was almost palpable. Men who one minute had a perception of manhood gleaned from a lifetime of movies, magazines and ungodly mentors, suddenly realized that true manhood really meant being like Jesus, the only Man Who ever lived exactly as God had created Him to live. Convicted of their lack of manliness, their "wimpiness" in following the crowd, men began to rush the stage to throw down vestiges of a man's life gone wrong—drugs, cigarettes, chains, keys to girlfriends' apartments, flasks of alcohol, lottery tickets, brass knuckles. In about fifteen minutes, the stage was littered with the symbols of worldly manhood.

Then the noise died down and the men began to sing. What a sound! It was as if the top had been lifted off that building and the sounds of a heavenly choir of male voices were wafting down from the corridors of Heaven.

There were no drums to beat, no scoreboard to read, but right there in the heart of Boston, right in the heart of Urban USA, men were set free. Free to be men!

There is no greater joy or fulfillment for any man than to be brought up to the level of Christlike manhood—"real" manhood.

This was just one day in those men's lives. What would they do from there? I know from experience, and from the hundreds of letters I receive, that men who grasp what real manhood is and begin to walk in that awareness—committing themselves to becoming real men each day—see a consistent, dramatic change in their lives from the very moment of their commitment.

Real manhood cannot be found in just a moment's emotional outburst. Neither is real manhood found in the image of physical prowess and handsomeness. Nor in personality, talent, intelligence, performance or profession. Real manhood is found within the heart of a man, the "inner man," his moral character, the "real man" that exudes beyond all external devices for the rest of the world to see.

Men cannot mature in moral distinctiveness with mere "head knowledge" or an "emotional catharsis," but we must constantly be evolving, purifying, changing the inmost parts of our beings. These inward elements create true quality in every part of life; not the exterior of a product, but the interior; not the polish on a chrome bumper, but the smooth purr of a well-tuned engine; not the talent on a ball field, but the citizenship and integrity when the spotlights go out. The quality of the inner man makes a man "real."

I was pastoring a church in San Bruno, California, just after World War II, when I began to learn what a real man is. Babies were "booming," former soldiers resumed their careers, suburbs sprang up, and congregations rapidly built and enlarged churches to accommodate everyone.

When Nancy and I accepted the church's call to ministry, only the unfinished shell of a building stood on the property. There were bare walls, a concrete floor and old wooden benches inside. We tried to remodel the building with volunteer labor, small amounts of cash and donated or used materials. Most of the volunteers were just that—they had little or no experience in the construction business but wanted to give their time. Scientists painted wood trim, teachers laid tile, preachers moved scaffolding, and homemakers nailed plywood. Everybody worked hard.

We did have a few genuine craftsmen, however. One of them was Paul, a contractor, carpenter and a craftsman of the highest degree. His woodwork was in great demand in San Francisco. During the week, he built high-quality (and high-priced) houses, but he spent his Saturdays helping us complete our building.

Paul's final task was to put a wooden veneer on the wall directly behind the sanctuary's pulpit. As he labored, the rest of us were awed by the difference his exquisite work made in our building. We were proud—thrilled that he had come to help us and eager to tell everyone of his accomplishments. So it came as a shock when, the day Paul finished, he took me aside and asked me not to tell anyone he had done the woodwork.

"Paul, why?" I asked. "You have worked so hard and done such a beautiful thing for us! I want to tell everyone what a great job you've done."

"Please don't," he said. "I'll show you why."

He proceeded to show me where the wood grain did not match exactly, where the miter was not perfectly joined, and the levels were off a fraction of an inch—things I would never have noticed if he had not pointed them out.

"I was glad to help," he said. "However, this work is not really up to my standard, and I would rather not have people know I did it."

Then he hit me with it.

"I could have done a better job if the material we used had been of better quality."

I never forgot that lesson: The quality of the product depends on the quality of the material used.

Its corollary is equally true: The cheaper the merchandise, the higher the gloss.

When the quality of the material is inferior, high gloss is necessary to camouflage the real product.

Furniture made from quality wood generally has only some polish to burnish

In the case of male identity and role, the answer is found in God as He revealed Himself on earth in the manhood of Jesus Christ.

it and bring out the excellence of the piece. However, furniture made from inferior woods generally has layers of lacquer or paint applied to give it a gloss that conceals the poor quality.

Knives made of tempered steel and a bone handle usually have nothing but a stamp on the blade designating the temper of the steel, and the bone is used in its natural state. However, knives made of plastic and pot metal most often have chrome on the blade and paint on the handle to give them a gloss that hides the cheap quality. The cheaper the merchandise, the higher the gloss.

True of furniture.

True of knives.

True of women ...

Prostitutes adorn themselves with flashy external accoutrements to hide the cheapness of their character. They put on layers of paint, clothing, cars, jewelry. High gloss for cheap merchandise.

... And true of men.

Con artists, whether in the ghetto or the executive board room, are slick and sophisticated, trying to impress people with outward show to disguise their fraudulent practices.

A man of cheap character always tries to associate with, gain identity from or control people of great talent or character. He vicariously draws upon others' identities to compensate for his own lack of integrity. Whatever he has is by association with others. Since his name is untrustworthy, he is always a name-dropper. By contrast, the quality of the material used in becoming a "real man" results in high quality.

A real man's strength of character can be relied upon. He doesn't defraud others for money, recognition or even the respect of his family. He is real in every area of life, in every facet of his being.

QUALITY MANHOOD

Every man is limited in life by three things:

(1) the knowledge of his own mind
(2) the worth of his own character
(3) the principles upon which he builds his own life[4]

These things shape a man within, for better or worse. They define the quality of his life. *Quality is always internal, not external.*

The quality of nations depends on the moral character of their people and the principles upon which they build their individual lives. The truth of this shines clearly in the history of Israel. They had a crisis in leadership and manhood that parallels ours today.

During the period of the judges, Gideon led Israel for a season. He died, leaving seventy sons. One was named Jotham. Governmental leaders crowned Jotham's half-brother, Abimelech, king and allowed him to kill all his brothers to secure the kingdom. Only Jotham escaped.

After the massacre, Jotham stood at a safe distance and called out the Parable of the Bramble Bush as an indictment against the leaders. In the parable, the olive, fig and grapevine all refused to become king of the trees because they were content with their private lives. So the trees asked the bramble bush to be king. The bramble accepted, but with arrogant demands that far exceeded its worth, saying the other trees must humble themselves and bow down beneath it or fire would come out of it to destroy them.[5]

Jotham used the parable to prophesy how Abimelech and his aides, who were to be the nation's leaders, would become enemies because they lacked the qualities necessary to lead. This story illustrates how qualified would-be leaders refuse public service because

The quality of the product depends on the quality of the material used. The cheaper the merchandise, the higher the gloss.

they are content with, and want to retain, their wealth and positions. Even today we find high-caliber men who won't serve in public office. Vain, ambitious men fill the leadership vacuum and arrogantly demand much from the people they are called to serve. The "Bramble Bush" problem has existed in every society, including ours.

In the U.S., some leaders cavort drunkenly in public, are indicted for illicit or immoral acts, engage in fraud and mismanagement, and yet maintain it is none of the public's business how they conduct themselves in private. *The truth is, whatever a man is in private—what he believes, practices and has built into his character—determines the actions and decisions he makes in public.*

Not just politicians, but some ministers need to correct the same erroneous thinking. *Private philosophy determines public performance.*

Not every man with character and integrity has the calling or capacity to serve in public office, but those who do must carefully consider the need, instead of flippantly dismissing the idea. The world depends on them.

One of the wisest men I ever met taught me a great lesson about the importance of building good character. I was a young man just starting out in ministry when Rev. W. T. Gaston, a greatly admired senior clergyman, came to help me with a visit to a wealthy woman. We were told she may be inclined to give a sizable offering toward a charity we worked with.

We met the rich, obese woman, sitting in a rocking chair in the living room of her comfortable home, surrounded by her many cats, who had the run of the place. In talking with her, we realized she was living a miserly existence, consumed with personal concern for her money and cats, had no intention of giving to a charity, and she let us know in no uncertain terms that her money was to be a legacy to her cats.

"What did you make of that?" I asked as we drove away.

"Well, Son," he said, "When the charm wears off, you have nothing but character left."

Charm is for the instant, character is constant.

Charm deals with the external, character with the internal. Charming manners that disguise a poor character will one day vanish, revealing the truth underneath.

One problem contributing to the crisis in men today is the reward system offered for presenting a great exterior. Cultural psychology advises: Present yourself well, and you'll be rewarded, regardless of your character (at least for a while).

The "problem" professional athletes of today promenaded through their colleges being lauded, compensated and rewarded for their talent, not their manhood. Once into the high-pressured world of professional sports, they do not have the inner strength to withstand the adversities, pressures and temptations confronting them. They use drugs, alcohol, gambling, violence and sex for escape, comfort, nurture and relief from tensions and anxieties. Many end up addicted and some even expelled from the sport they love. By contrast, some of the great athletes of all time we remember because of their charity, citizenship and integrity.

Fame can come in a moment, but greatness comes with longevity. I spoke on this topic at a National Football League team chapel. The head coach quoted it to the press the next day, and his quotation went out on the Associated Press wire service. A year later, a sportscaster repeated it on television. They remember it and repeat it because they recognize its validity in the sports world. It's true in every way. Greatness comes over the course of time. Those becoming real men build not on what they can gain from the moment, but on what will benefit for life. *Life is composed of our choices, constructed by our words and revealed by our character.*

PITCH PERSONALITY, BUILD CHARACTER

Consider Abraham and Lot. When God called Abraham out from Ur of the Chaldees, Abraham took along his nephew Lot, and they traveled to a new land. Standing on a hillside and looking across a valley, Abraham gave Lot first choice of the land. Lot looked at the well-watered, verdant orchards and the alabaster-white houses in the valley before him and chose it over the rock-strewn mountains. But behind those alabaster-white walls, and lying in the midst of those lush fields, lay the wicked cities of Sodom and Gomorrah.

Abraham chose what Lot rejected, the terrain of Canaan with all its unproven but promised worth and value. Years later, when Abraham was prospering and Lot had moved inside the city limits of Sodom, Abraham had to rescue Lot, and intercede with God to send angels to rescue Lot again just before the destruction of Sodom and Gomorrah.[6] Lot's pivotal choice sprang from his day-to-day decisions.

The Bible recounts that everywhere Abraham went, he pitched his tents and built his altars. He concentrated on the permanent issues of life, constructed his character and developed a lasting relationship with God. He understood the transient status of life. Lot, however, built an altar only after irreparable harm had come to him and his family.

In a perverted society, men "pitch" their altars and "build" their tents. In other words, they "pitch" their character and "build" their personality. Wrong strategy. Poor results.

Build your character on the foundation of truth, use faithfulness as its cornerstone, making righteousness its walls, and your good character will be known by all. Good character will stand the test of time.

Trying to develop a godly character apart from God will fail. Developing Christlikeness from a heart turned toward God will cause a man to stand for all eternity. God alone makes this so. We go as far as we can in ourselves, but ultimately, God must make up the difference for us. This is why Jesus had to die for our sins, for we could not compensate for our own lack of godliness.

When the charm wears off, you have nothing but character left.

Jesus said that only God was "good" and that He did only those things God told Him to do. We must study Jesus' character and attributes, our model of "real" manhood, to discover how to become the men God created us to be. More than putting on a veneer of Christlike manhood, Jesus' character and attributes must be rooted deep within us, so we can grow in our relationship with Him.

Becoming a real man requires an ongoing, purifying change in the inmost parts of a man's being. Only God knows the hearts of men. We can depend on Him to reveal our hearts to us, to do a purifying work within us and cause us to become Christlike—"real men."

We live in a world that tries to accomplish life's superior purposes with inferior ways. We must reject second-rate substitutes and contend with things that are real.

2

The Substitute Society

TWO YEARS AGO MY WIFE NANCY AND I SPENT A delightful week in Vienna, Austria, just before Christmas. We saw the great statues of national heroes, massive ancient buildings abutting the street with their frescoes and pilasters, holiday-decked streets and roadways winding around the magnificent Blue Danube. The Christmas lights lit up amid celebration and song. Christmas left no corner of the city untouched.

And yet, one thing was missing. Jesus! The cause of the celebration. The people had lost the very reason for the festivity itself. Santa Claus was heralded as the substitute for the Christ. More than forty years after my eyes opened to the reality of Jesus, this human blindness still amazes me.

Christmas isn't the only time we are a "substitute society." Artificial sweetener, artificial insemination, sperm banks, surrogate mothers, even the holiday decorations we enjoy each year are part of the substitute society we live in. The genuine article is replaced by things of similar, but often inferior, quality. We substitute cubic zirconium for diamonds, vinyl for leather, synthetics for silk, plastic for wood, the counterfeit for the real. A fast-growing trend in plastic surgery today is "muscle implants" for people who don't (won't) exercise.

Some substitutes are valid and necessary, others are dangerous and ruinous. Substituting relative values for absolutes in moral life can be devastating.

Some historians call us a "plastic people." Ecologists scream for attention to what they call a "throwaway" society. The word "value" itself has lost its meaning. *We often throw away people and keep things.*

WHAT VALUES?

During the 1960s, a group of social scientists developed a teaching method called "Values Clarification," the process of determining what may or may not be right for a person in any given situation. In this scenario, all moral "oughts" are reduced from universal, absolute values to individual, relative values. What's right for me may not be right for you, but that's okay. The social scientists claimed it was a way to teach values to school-aged children without taking any specific moral position. The basic philosophy behind the teaching is that no absolute values exist, or, as its proponents put it, values are "personal things."

Educators were taught that it was wrong to instruct children that murder and stealing are bad. Teaching that honesty and loyalty are good was equally wrong. They said the teacher should do no more than help the student clarify his own values. Mr. Baer, an associate professor at New York State College, wrote in the *Wall Street Journal* that "values clarification" in essence, gave the message to adolescents that parents, the school or society had no right to tell them what standards should guide their behavior, especially sexually.

Bill Murray—son of the infamous atheist Madelyn Murray O'Hare who fought, and won, against school prayer in the U.S.—wrote a tract on "values clarification." After being dragged unwillingly through courtrooms during his school days, Bill now fights to undo what his mother did to public schools. Murray concludes, "We must return moral instruction to our schools. *Absolute right and absolute wrong do exist.*"[1]

Society has substituted relativism for absolutes and has perverted our values. The values of our society are reflected in "our heroes, what we spend our money on, what we watch

Many of those caught up in our substitute society claim that bad is good and good is bad, deceiving themselves into living a lie rather than embracing truth.

on TV," according to *Newsweek* journalist Nicols Fox.
She stated:

> It's not so much that [the church's] moral leadership is
> being ignored as that, to a great extent, they've abdicated
> the role. Collectively, they seem to exude the same rela-
> tivism and insecurity about right and wrong as the rest
> of us.[2]

She concluded that the society as a whole has been left
yearning for absolutes.

Columnist William Murchison points out that the
Protestant work ethic is "on its last legs." At one time, we
believed in "hard work, paying debts, staying married, obey-
ing our parents and going to church." But according to
Murchison, today people say:

> Yuk! So early twentieth century ... And so successful in
> nurturing the habits that bound families together, that
> kept the streets safe, that engendered trust, responsibility
> and social peace. Were the old days better than the new
> days? Of course they were! Not perfect; just better.[3]

A recent survey of more than seven hundred British
youth, aged seventeen to twenty-four, revealed that they valued conformity above rebellion. Shocked researchers found
that the average respondent spent nearly six hours a week in
bars and spent one-fifth of his or her weekly income there.
"For young men, drinking and getting drunk is an important
social ritual."[4] They conform to the values they hold.

The practice of substitution leads to perverted philosophies and practices that display blatant inconsistencies.
Many of those caught up in our substitute society claim that
bad is good and good is bad, deceiving themselves into living a lie rather than embracing truth.[5] In doing so, they try
to justify their inconsistencies.

Today, most humanists oppose the death penalty for
murder but fight for the right to murder unborn children.

How inconsistent! Letting the guilty go free but destroying the innocent.

It is easier for some to try to make God in their image, rather than to conform themselves to His image.[6] The New Age movement proliferates in churches that worship a god of their own making rather than submit to the leadership of Christ. Such cults demand that God conform to their lifestyle rather than make their lifestyles conform to God's Word.

It's easier to bring homosexuality out of the closet than to clean the closet. Yet, while the secularists "come out of the closet," they want to push Christians into one. In 1988, Tim Robertson wrote:

> Many today are following an agenda that Lenin spoke of decades ago when he said he would not speak of being an atheist, but rather would speak of religion as being an entirely private matter. His strategy was to promote the concept that people are free to express religion if done so in a purely private matter. To many people, this sounds harmless enough, but the net effect, however, is to strip Christianity from the public arena. Liberal members of Congress and the secular media are now combining in an effort to force Christianity into the realm of "private expression."[7]

Intellectuals, whose work changed the philosophies that undergird our society, display incredible inconsistencies in their own lives. Karl Marx, the self-professed liberator of humanity, used racist slurs against a political opponent and altered his research findings to make it fit his thesis in *Das Kapital*.[8] Jean Jacques Rousseau, whose *Social Contract* promoted justice in politics, and whose *Emile* proposed a new order of education, sent his own five children to a home for foundlings.[9] A journalist for

> Some religious people are not necessarily apathetic or lacking in energy—they are simply indifferent to the Word of God.

U.S. News & World Report editorialized: "The old affluent, liberal elites spoke left but lived right. And the people of Middle America paid."[10]

Many who shape our way of thinking don't live by their own philosophies. The irony is that many reporters, who tar-and-feather preachers for having incomes that exceed what they think is correct, will laud lewd and perverse performers who make millions. Certainly, some ministers are guilty of excess or lust, but the media's reporting practices indicate a desire to drag Christianity down to their level rather than face the conviction of the Holy Spirit in their own lives. *Those who want to be real men must seek to live on a higher level and recognize these substitution tendencies, bracing ourselves with truth and reality.*

THE REAL WORLD

Jesus *is* truth. Therefore, Jesus *is* reality.

I was leaving a Christian men's event one day after several hundred men had experienced a powerful movement of God. One man said to me, "Well, it's back to the real world now."

"What do you mean?" I asked. "This *was* the real world! Everything else hinges on what just happened here!"

We cannot be deceived into believing that the circumstances of life are the sum total of our existence on earth. To do so is to cut ourselves off from the reality of the supernatural and the truth that we were created as spiritual beings. Real men recognize truth and cling to it. Unlike the Pharisees of Jesus' day, who substituted religion for relationship, real men recognize Truth, submit to Truth and are discipled by Him Who is called Truth.

"Secular Pharisees" today justify every inconsistency that finds its way into society. They are like those Jesus addressed centuries ago: "For John the Baptist came neither eating bread nor drinking wine, and you say, 'He has a demon.' The Son of Man has come eating and drinking, and you say, 'Look, a glutton and a winebibber, a friend of tax collectors and sinners!'"[11]

Men make substitutions in the most intimate parts of their lives—their relationships—then wonder why difficulties beset them. Consider two of these:

- **Money for affection:** Many men would rather give their wives the checkbook than a warm embrace or loving kiss. It's simply easier to give money than oneself.
- **Things for time:** Many men would rather buy their children things than spend time with them, even though the giving of self is the evidence of love.[12]

Real men must understand that substitutions are not originals. The Church has also made substitutions and, in doing so, lost much of the essence of biblical wisdom, which is vital for a vigorous, productive people. In the Christian community, people substitute:

- **Talent for anointing:** Relying on the external rather than the internal. We must realize that God commits to character, not talent.
- **Remorse for repentance:** Sorrow for getting caught is not sorrow for having sinned. Human sorrow and godly sorrow are as far apart as Hell and Heaven.[13]
- **Traditions for commandments:** Churchianity and Christianity are incompatible. The Lord Jesus Christ rebuked those who substituted the traditions of men for the commandments of God.[14]
- **Respectability for righteousness:** We are not saved by our culture but by the blood of Christ. Some people are better by nature than others are by grace. Natural graces are no substitute for saving grace.
- **Passion for obedience:** Mistaking a mere emotional experience with God as a genuine love of God can cost you your soul. The evidence of love is obedience to the Word. If the Word of God does not have lordship in your life, then Christ is not Lord of your life.[15]
- **Status symbols for relationships:** Stained-glass windows or spiritual exercises in religious life can never substitute for a vital relationship with a living Lord.

Some religious people are not necessarily apathetic or lacking in energy—they are simply indifferent to the Word of God.[16] Indifference is often a form of rebellion. Ezekiel the prophet suffered such an affront. The people who came to hear him were indicted by the Lord when He told Ezekiel, "You are very entertaining to them, like someone who sings lovely songs with a beautiful voice or plays well on an instrument. They hear what you say but don't pay any attention to it!"[17]

The "rich young ruler" of Jesus' day faced the decision to love God or money. Money won.[18] Hundreds of years before, Ezekiel pegged religious people: "They talk very sweetly about loving the Lord, but with their hearts they are loving their money."[19] They heard the Word but refused to act on it.[20] Jesus warned: "Not everyone who says to Me, 'Lord, Lord,' shall enter into the kingdom of heaven."[21] *Substituting confession for commitment can be damning.*

The Church was once the driving force behind politics, social reform and moral values. It was the central focus and meeting place for whole cities. But our substitutions have led to an isolated, inferior Church without the status in the community it formerly commanded.

We preach humility but practice inferiority. We preach separation but practice isolation. Holiness requires separation from the world, but isolation results in losing our impact on the world. Humility and holiness further the work of the Church in the world, inferiority and isolation destroy it.

We substitute works for faith, programs for worship, individual experiences for continued abiding, the instant for the constant, culture for salvation. Many men today substitute remorse for repentance, thinking they are mollifying a jealous God. The merely religious, thinking they do service to God only at church, seek out other things to satisfy their deepest cravings: possessions, power or prestige.

I will never forget the evening Nancy and I dropped in on some friends whose children were now grown and had come home to visit. We caught up on the children, what they were doing, where they were. As we left that evening, I remember hitting my fist on the steering wheel of the car in frustration and sorrow. I told Nancy, "Every one of them talked about the new homes, yachts, sports their children are enjoying—but not one of the children know Jesus as Savior. They are substituting culture for salvation."

Back in the times of the kings of Israel, Rehoboam, through compromise, weakened the nation, allowing their enemy to raid the Temple, taking the shields of gold from it. Rehoboam then substituted brass shields for the gold.[22] It was an external evidence of an internal change in relationship to God. Like him, we can substitute the human for the divine, good for best, respectability for righteousness.

Perhaps the greatest substitution error in the Church is substituting God's unconditional love for His conditional promises. We chafe at the word *if* in scriptural promises. We are uncomfortable with meeting God's conditions to receive His blessings, like children who fret at having to meet conditions before they can receive the parents' reward. But to obtain the results of conditional promises, we must meet the conditions.

Thank God, for if His promises were unconditional and His love conditional, salvation would be impossible. Our salvation is not based on our goodness, but on His gracious, unconditional love.

In our substitutions, we lose the opportunity to satisfy the yearnings of the inner man for true peace in the heart. God said, "I will give them a heart to know Me,"[23] and He sent Jesus into the world to accomplish that relationship.

Intimate relationship is the heart-cry and God's goal for every life. Christ prayed that we might be one with the Father, knowing Him intimately as He did. God has lovingly given of Himself to enable humans to be His friends. Jesus makes it possible for us to have His righteousness, truth, Spirit and power that we might enter into a right relationship with Him.

While society is hooked on substitutes, real men go for the real thing—Christlikeness!

3

Cracks in the Mirror

"MIRROR, MIRROR, ON THE WALL, WHO IS THE fairest of them all?" cried the wicked witch. But when an answer came that put her second on the list, she wanted to kill number one—Snow White.

Today we still compete for the top spot, but the rules have changed. Reality doesn't matter. Image, however, does. Television ads boast "image is everything," but the images projected in mainstream society bypass the real issues of life.

Many men are content to become shadows without substance, elevating talent and ignoring character. Lost in a blizzard of confused images, they thrust themselves forward with pretense, a "pretend" image, trying to convince the world they are something they know they are not, hoping that somehow they will strike upon the right path before they are discovered as imposters. When the pressure catches up, rehabilitation and counseling will target behaviors triggered by the internal struggle, but core issues must be addressed.

The image is not everything. A man can go for the image or the stuff of life behind the image. The results are a fabricated man or a real man.

Every man has three identities to deal with: the man he wants others to think he is; the man he thinks he is; and the man he really is. The degree to which these three coincide determines the depth of real manhood and the amount of peace in one's life.

THE MAN HE WANTS OTHERS TO THINK HE IS

Self-help books offer advice on convincing others that a man is something other than what he is. Businessmen are advised to build a strong image. Advertising agencies earn millions of dollars generating a client's image to attract customers. Publicity firms spend clients' hard-earned cash to create, protect and project an image, often to conceal a true identity.

Image is big business. *Right or wrong, image works!*

Today, men and nations are trying to recreate depictions of high government officials because of the difficulties in gaining credibility. These are dream jobs for public relations firms who bolster tarnished images.

In his book, *A Question of Character*, Thomas C. Reeves assessed former U.S. President John F. Kennedy as a man who lacked greatness but had great public relations: "While he had ample courage and at times showed considerable prudence, he was deficient in integrity, compassion, and temperance."[1] He reveals John Kennedy as a sexually immoral man. His proclivity for promiscuity is now chronicled in the pages of history, as well as in scandal and gossip magazines, but the world's moral level has fallen so low that his licentiousness is accepted with impunity.

The book, *Silent Coup*, and others give a sordid picture of men at the pinnacle of political power as deceitful, unethical, liars, unscrupulous, base and ominous in their danger to the very country they swore to uphold.[2]

Americans as a people have even suffered a terrible beating—blighted by Vietnam and Watergate, shattered during the Iranian hostage crisis, diminished as terrorists targeted us. American leadership was challenged throughout the world. Then, through a series of events—hosting a heralded Olympics, staging successful military operations, advancing free enterprise in Communist countries—the American image improved in

> A man can go for the image or the stuff of life behind the image. The results are a fabricated man or a real man.

the minds of its citizens. The restoration of the image of prosperity, patriotism and productivity became the basis for an overwhelming success in the Gulf War and a great sense of unity and national pride.

A good image works in private life as well. Robert helped me in the early days of my work with men. He had taken his father's company to a greater degree of success than ever before, but he left the firm for a couple of years to improve his image in his dad's eyes. Until Robert earned success elsewhere, his father treated him as though he were a boy. Robert's success in another firm shattered the image his father held and created a new concept of him in his father's mind. Robert returned, and his dad trusted him with the responsibility he was capable of handling, something that never could have happened until the change in image occurred.

Perhaps one of the best illustrations of this came when God intervened in individual and corporate life to elevate a person to leadership. Moses delivered Israel from Egypt, led the Israelites through their desert meanderings, brought supernatural provision to the people and was a proven commander, conqueror and champion of the people. Then Moses died, and Joshua became the country's leader. He had served Moses faithfully, discharged his duties willingly and honored God. However, to take leadership of a people that even God found truculent, *Joshua needed to be seen in a different light than that which was reflected by his relationship to Moses.*

"The Lord magnified Joshua in the sight of all Israel; and they feared him, as they had feared Moses, all the days of his life,"[3] the Bible records. The magnification process changed the image of Joshua in the people's minds. Their new perception enabled Joshua to exercise authority, which he would not have enjoyed, had they thought of him only as Moses' associate. Joshua's value in their eyes increased according to their

> True integrity is found only in a man's character, not in his company brochure or in what he calls himself.

perception of him. Every successor to a leader must be given new esteem, greater regard and standing to enable him to begin his task.

Images are as important to the illicit as to the legitimate. Newport Beach, California, has been dubbed the "scam capital" of America. Deceitful would-be executives extort fortunes presenting worthless stocks, nonexistent products and other ephemeral deals by using eye-grabbing graphics, glossy stationery, authoritative titles and pretentious addresses to present the image of a successful, legitimate corporation.

Lost moral values in the 1920s spurred the stock market crash and Great Depression. The same loss of values in the 1980s created a financial crisis that will cause suffering for two generations, and could yet cause a worldwide economic disaster. Loss of integrity, ethics, faithfulness, trustworthiness and character are behind it. Ironically, *integrity* is a new buzzword in business.

True integrity is found only in a man's character, not in his company brochure or in what he calls himself. This is what separates real men from those with merely the image of manliness.

Larry is a self-styled financier whose father is a minister. He grew up in a godly home with praying parents, but never built his life on a solid foundation of righteous principles, genuine faith, and personal relationship with Jesus Christ. A man of tremendous talent and charismatic charm, he built an image, but never developed the substance of godly character.

Larry impressed a young man named John with his contacts. John invested in Larry's projects and encouraged others to do likewise. The investors didn't see that Larry's personal charm covered up a deceitful character. John and the investors lost everything but Larry was impervious to their plight. His dad, mother and wife lamely excused away his behavior and glossed over what happened.

The Bible warns not to associate with one who calls himself a "brother" but is an extortioner or swindler.[4]

When John and the other investors lost every dime, John awakened to the fact he had been conned through a carefully constructed image. John's chagrin was not prompted just by his loss, but the huge losses of those he counseled. To John it was a financial rape, and he suffered the consequences. It took him years to recover, while Larry continued his conniving ways with different, unsuspecting people. Larry derived his ability to con people from imitating, not building, the godly character of his parents.

John's misguided counsel to the investors illustrates another important biblical truth: *Counselors determine the destiny of kings.*

The life of Rehoboam, successor to his father King Solomon, illustrates this. When Rehoboam became king, Jeroboam confronted him at the behest of the people to ask for a financial relief by lowering their taxes. Rehoboam took up the issue with the aged, wise, experienced men who had served Solomon. They counseled him to lower taxes so that he might serve a lifetime as king.

Rehoboam then turned to the young men ascending to power with him, who were ambitious, inexperienced, vying for power, position and prestige, and eager to give an answer pleasing to the king. They said to tell the people he was king now, not his father, and that the tax burden would be worse, not better. Rehoboam followed the advice of inexperienced, avaricious young men, which resulted in the loss of favor, stature, authority, money and divided his kingdom. He never regained the control he had dreamed of.[5]

Rehoboam's counselors determined his destiny.

THE MAN HE THINKS HE IS

Take the principle of counsel, add the understanding of the power of images, and you have a combustible combination. Rehoboam may have believed he was someone other than who he was, based on the input of those around him. Brad is a man I once knew well who succumbed to this. Believing in an image of himself that was not based on reality was his undoing.

Brad started a business with little more than an idea. Over the years it expanded beyond his expectations. Many trustworthy friends who started the business with him eventually moved on. New faces were brought in by new executives, some of questionable character. The quality of people around him changed from those who shared his dream to those who saw an opportunity to benefit themselves.

Brad took financial advice from those who were now close to him. Some gave good counsel, but opportunists knew they could not enrich themselves until Brad had gained more than they wanted. In their lusts, they told Brad how great he was, what he was worth, what he should have, and encouraged him to draw more for himself, at the expense of the company.

With a new image of himself created by these seducers, Brad began to engage in fiscal manipulations, taking monies for himself that were not his. As he enriched himself, he was willing to pay his counselors what they wanted. After some financial audits, Brad was indicted, sentenced, went to jail, lost many of his possessions, and endured public disgrace.

His counselors moved on to find new positions and advance their careers. Their counsel was not based on what was good for Brad, but on what was good for them. Brad suffered the consequences, while they reaped the dividends.

We are motivated to become the image we see of ourselves. As a man thinks, so he is. *Creating a positive image is one of the most powerful things a man can do. Shattering an image is one of the most devastating.*

Books, movies and real lives repeat the story of immature males who are bound to an image created in younger years. Their identity crisis, which must be resolved to reach maturity, is really an image crisis. Athletes, hopelessly clinging to "glory days," cheat themselves out of the glory of growing wise and maturing as they age.

We can cover our nature by projecting an image we want others to believe, or we can have our nature changed by identifying ourselves with the person of Jesus Christ.

"The glory of young men is their strength; of old men, their experience," Proverbs states.[6]

According to the Apostle Peter, whatever overcomes a man, "by him also he is brought into bondage."[7] Men are held in bondage by false images that overcome them. Such images form the basis for idolatry in life.

The way to resist false images of ourselves is by thinking correctly, which comes from "renewing your mind" as the Word of God permeates your thought life and the life of Christ permeates your being.

THE MAN HE REALLY IS

The image of real manhood is found in God, Who created all human beings in His image. The knowledge of God is found in church. The Church desperately needs real men to teach that knowledge to floundering men and teen-men. Yet, the mores of society impose themselves on the Church, rather than the Church setting the standard for the world.

During recent strife within one denomination, a church official publicly advised that "the Bible is obsolete and too paternalistic. Culture should set our standards, not Scripture." How arrogant! How foolish! Allowing culture to create the blueprint for human behavior is like trying to build the Empire State Building on the ocean. Cultural values change with the times, unless they are built on an absolute standard. And without moral absolutes, everything becomes relative. Relatives are as unhelpful as an unanchored buoy for someone lost at sea.

End-times Bible scholars have prophesied for years that people will one day bow in worship to the "image of the beast."[8] That image was thought of as some statue, icon, or monument. Now we realize people can be deceived into worshiping some symbol, logo, or concept created by modern-day "image makers."

The image of the "beast" or "system" will one day be projected so that the minds of men and women will embrace its philosophy, and their hearts will be enslaved to its rule.

The truth behind that image will be evil, but the image it will project will be one of peace, hope and concern for others.

With the confused images in the world, the power behind the images, and the knowledge that one day the entire world will be deceived into believing a lying image, men must come to an understanding of the most critical true image of reality—the image in which they were created—God's image. That's an image worthy of emulation. It can change our inner man.

PROFANING THE WORD

Men and nations are not great by virtue of their wealth, but by the wealth of their virtues.

"Out of [the heart] spring the issues of life."[9] Moral character, which denotes real manhood, emanates from the inner core of a man's being, his heart. And the man who has revealed that character most completely and consistently is Jesus Christ.

Jesus came to earth as the express image of God. He knew in whose image He was created, and Who He represented. As such, He was secure in His identity. Because He is "real," men who find themselves in Him discover true security in identification with Him. He, in turn, begins to reshape them into His perfect image.

Jesus is called the "Word" of God. Words are the expression of a man's nature, just as God's Word is the expression of His nature. "In the beginning was the Word, and the Word was with God, and the Word was God."[10] Christ came as the Word incarnate. He was the very expression of God to all people.[11]

Our words say volumes about our character. Profanity is an attitude or condition of heart that breaks God's commandment, "You shall not take the Name of the Lord your God in vain."[12] As morality wanes in public life, profanity proliferates. One can hardly shop for a birthday card or read a journal without being confronted with profane words.

Taking the Name of the Lord in vain can be done both in word and action. Esau was a "profane person" because he traded his God-given birthright for a bowl of stew.[13] He was willing to take his eternal inheritance and trade it for material substance—substituting sacred for secular, spiritual for temporal.

Profaning the Name of the Lord can be done in other ways. Say, for example, a friend in Cleveland calls me and says he has just met my wife. My reply is that Nancy has not been in Cleveland. Come to find out the woman he met is an imposter to whom I have never spoken nor given permission to use my name. I find her and ask why she is using my name.

"I like the way you talk, so I just started calling myself Mrs. Cole," she says, or, "I asked a friend, and she said it was all right if I used your name."

By assuming my name immorally and illegally, without my authority or permission, she is profaning my name—taking my name in vain.

Think of how people can do the same thing with Jesus. Many call themselves Christians without ever having a personal relationship with Jesus Christ. They do not understand that no one but Christ Himself has the right to give permission to bear His Name.

When a person repents of sin, believes on Jesus Christ, is "born of His Spirit" and establishes a personal relationship with Jesus Christ, he or she then has the right to be called a Christian. Taking that Name by any other means is to profane His Name. Christ has reserved this right for Himself.

We can cover our nature by projecting an image we want others to believe, or we can have our nature changed by identifying ourselves with the person of Jesus Christ. Then we are "reborn" as men who are truly made in the "image of God."

But who is this Jesus, anyway? Let's take a close look.

Part 2

The Real Man

4

Behold the Man

ECCE HOMO! "BEHOLD THE MAN!"

Jesus was "found in appearance as a man."[1] Whatever else Jesus was, He was a Man. God the Father declared Him to be the "Son of Man." Jesus was presented in His hour of trial as *the* Real Man!

Pilate, the governor of Roman-occupied Israel, announced to the world that he had seen a real man.[2] He had seen many men in crisis before his tribunal, seen their character unveiled as pressure melted all pretense. But Pilate viewed Jesus with awe and respect.

Pilate looked for a way to avoid the demands of the crowd, but he was political to the core—an expert in compromise, always doing the expedient to maintain position and power. He bowed to the people, after giving his thoughts and feelings.

"I find no fault in him,"[3] Pilate declared.

Pilate washed his hands before the angry multitude that cried for crucifixion, showing the religious leaders and the people that he wanted no part of that blood on his hands.[4] Pilate then had "King of the Jews" written in Latin, Greek and Hebrew, announcing Who Jesus was.[5] These were the languages of government, culture and religion.

Jesus was born in a manger, grew up in a carpenter's home and worked in the shop. He lived the life of a peasant, yet with royal demeanor. He had no home of His own during His ministry, yet rarely lacked lodging or food. He died upon a cross as a government enemy and was buried in a borrowed tomb. Throughout His walk on this earth, He carried the realization of a purpose greater than life itself.

For thirty years He prepared for three years of public ministry. When He spoke of the virtue of patience, He had lived it. Never premature, either in action or speech, He waited. *Patience is the virtue of preparation.*

His "life was the light of men."[6] His path one of righteousness, His work marked by eternity. He showed all of this and more in His every utterance, attitude and influence.

Jesus Christ was the most virile and vital of men. Rather than the soft, spineless, wimpish, docile man so often painted in word and picture, He was a man's man. He could act with great gentleness and genuine compassion toward a widow, the sick or the needy. But when confronted by bigotry and hypocrisy, His white-hot anger could blaze with righteous indignation.

When He saw the Father's house of worship defiled by dishonest "money-changers," with indignation He drove them out and sought to restore His Father's house to a place of prayer.[7]

Jesus' wisdom confounded religious scholars, rebuked legalists and revealed the true nature of God as Father to those who believed on Him. He told the religious leaders that their insincerity and hypocrisy would keep them from Heaven while repentant publicans and harlots would be welcomed in. The Pharisees were excoriated as "whitewashed tombs," "serpents," and "vipers," because they prayed long and loud in public, but in private, they stole from the aged and weak.[8]

Confronted by religious zealots, eager to show their sanctimonious piety, He exposed their true nature. They dragged a woman before Him, caught in the "very act of adultery," insisting on stoning her. (My first question would have been, "How did you know where to find her?")

He said, "He who is without sin among you, let him throw a stone at

> **Jesus Christ was the most virile and vital of men. Rather than the soft, spineless, wimpish, docile man so often painted in word and picture, He was a man's man.**

her first."[9] One by one, they backed away, leaving the woman standing alone with Jesus. She was a great sinner, but she stood in the presence of a great Savior. Jesus quietly and graciously said, "Neither do I condemn you; go and sin no more."[10]

A Man of grace, chivalry and gentleness to the needy, Jesus' acute sense of right and wrong left Him unafraid to rebuke others, regardless of their status or stature. Confronted by cynicism and disbelief in His hometown, He remained undaunted. "No prophet is accepted in his own country" was His perception of the indignity.[11]

He was not afraid of people. They rejected His anointing that equipped Him for ministry, so He merely passed through the midst of them. The splendor of His person was such that no man dared touch Him.[12]

CALM, ASSURED DIGNITY

The perfect balance of Jesus' life revealed a dignity unrivaled by any other historical figure, before or after Him. His strengths, revealed in His relationships, first found their basis in the security of His identity. *Jesus knew who He was, what He was about and what He was to accomplish.*

Jesus never lost His composure. He suffered the most humiliating indignities ever heaped on anyone. But even from the cross, He looked down through incredible pain, saw His mother and tenderly told John to take care of her.[13]

Jesus' wisdom confounded religious scholars, rebuked legalists and revealed the true nature of God as Father to those who believed on Him.

Never disconcerted by human opposition, improper or offensive action or attitude, Jesus never acted hastily or foolishly. He was poised and balanced. There was a finish and completion about Him that caused men to admire Him and women to respect Him.

Jesus' greatest source of preparation was prayer. When others demanded action, He was patient in prayer. He knew the Kingdom He was building would continue long after He left the earth and must be built according to the Father's will. His submission to the Father took place in prayer before it evolved into deeds. Jesus knew better than anyone what it meant to "move the arm of God in prayer."

Intercession was not an activity for Jesus but a way of life. To assure Himself of right decisions, He spent entire nights in prayer.[14] In preparation for His greatest trial at Calvary, He prayed until His pores bled, with blood like sweat from His brow. The intensity of His prayer life is forever understood from that long, lonely night in Gethsemane.[15]

Jesus knew our strengths and frailties, our possibilities and limits. His management techniques were designed to develop the maximum potential of those who followed Him. His training abilities were of such great caliber that His students altered the course of world history.

Whenever Jesus spoke, His counsel was not scattered, vague or inept. He declared truth. To the rich, selfish and covetous, He said that it was easier for a camel to go through the eye of a needle than for them to get into Heaven.[16] Even Peter felt the sting of truth when Jesus said, "Get behind Me, Satan!"[17]

Though viewing the world collectively, Jesus took care of people individually. His eternal philosophical perspective might be espoused one minute, and the next He could spend time with a mother and her baby. Simplicity and humility marked His life. *Jesus was never too busy to meet the needs of those who came to Him.*

Jesus stated to the religious world that social action toward the needy was taken on His behalf. "Inasmuch as you did it [acts of kindness] to one of the least of these [the hungry, naked, sick, imprisoned, and strangers] My bretheren, you did it to Me."[18] It was a bold, brave and gallant declaration in the face of those whose only concern was their self-conceived sense of righteousness.[19]

Jesus' love knew no bounds and His forgiveness no limits.

Modern-day humanitarians did not invent social consciousness. Jesus did, and He made it a bedrock component of the Church. Throughout the world, the greatest acts of charity, monies invested, lives sacrificed, have come from men and women who accept the will of God for their lives in carrying out the commands of Christ.

Jesus' love knew no bounds and His forgiveness no limits.

When taking His last supper with His disciples, He noticed that they didn't exhibit the common courtesy of washing the feet of guests. Nobody had offered to wash His feet. Rather than rebuke them for their oversight, He took pail and towel and, in humility, began to wash their feet.[20]

Jesus taught that a man is only qualified to lead to the degree he is willing to serve.[21]

Peter tried to rebuke the Lord for attempting such a servile, menial, and humble task. But Peter needed the lesson in humility.[22] *True nobility is realized in true humility.*

Humility is not found in self-demeaning attitudes or speech, but in the willingness to be anonymous. *Anonymity is the essence of humility.*

Jesus repeatedly instructed those He healed and helped not to tell others what had happened.[23] He wanted all glory to be given to the Father.[24] He came to give glory to the Father, knowing that the Holy Spirit would glorify Him when the Spirit came to dwell in His followers. His time was not yet come, He constantly said.[25]

Jesus didn't just teach people, He trained them. To train others, you must invest time, give of yourself, impart understanding, develop skills and motivate them to lead others.

What Jesus accomplished in three brief years has spanned the pages of history, rewritten the story of humanity and given eternal meaning to every human life. Because of the redemptive nature of His work and the nature of His person, often Christ's manhood is minimized.

Intercession was not an activity for Jesus but a way of life.

Look at the great men of history—whose accomplishments in the arts, literature, science, commerce, music, government and religion are posted in national archives. Yet which of them has established a moral kingdom that will never end? That Christ did, and is still doing, as testified to by the sacrificial devotion and moral victory of people who continue following Him today. Two thousand years from now, Jesus will still rule and reign in people's hearts, whether in earth or Heaven. No one will ever do what this one single Man has done.

That Jesus established His Kingdom on earth by the moral perfection of His life, and proved Himself the "power of God to salvation,"[26] is beyond controversy to those who believe. To those who do not believe, He is the most controversial figure in human history.

The reverence created by His person exalts Him, giving Him a Name above every name. One day He will cause every knee to bow before Him and every tongue to confess He is Lord to the glory of the Father.[27]

Noble yet humble, dignified yet unassuming, gracious yet indignant at injustice, tender yet tough, holy yet human, confrontational yet compassionate, truthful yet understanding and filled with wisdom, Jesus exemplified all that is best in humanity. He is the epitome of real manhood.

5

The Power of Life

COMMUNICATION IS THE BASIS OF LIFE.

Agreement is the power of life.

Exchange is the process of life.

Balance is the key to life.

These four principles that every man needs to understand are essential to life.

Communication. Without the Bible telling us of Jesus, we would be eternally bereft of God's grace. His Spirit communicates to us that we are God's children.

The earth, animals and people alike establish some form of communication as a prelude to reproduction. Communication of the sun's power to earth causes plant photosynthesis that produces organic food for human consumption. Pollen is carried by wind, insects, water and other agents to impregnate plants and produce seeds.

Business, education and marriage are based on proper communication. Without it, knowledge would cease. Due to new methods of communication, we live in an information age, a shrinking world and a global community.

When communication stops, abnormality sets in, and the ultimate abnormality is death. A flower derives its existence from the sap flowing from the roots of a plant. When it is severed from its stem, abnormality sets in. Without reconciliation, the ultimate end of the flower is death. Likewise, when communication stops between married partners, the result is often divorce, which is a form of death.

Agreement. Agreement is the power of life because, without it, both authority and ability would be lost. Marriage is based on two parties agreeing to live together until death parts them. Developers are restricted from building unless they are in agreement with all parties and civic authorities.

Likewise, until humans agree with God's assessment of them and His provision for their eternal benefit, they are without His authority and ability. As they live in agreement with His Word by faith, His power is released in their lives.

"A house divided cannot stand," Jesus said.[1]

"Unite my heart to fear Your name," cried the Psalmist.[2]

Disagreement produces powerlessness, agreement produces power.

Companies with employees in agreement with their policies, united in a common effort, produce great profits. With disunity, confusion and misunderstanding, productivity is lost.

Exchange. The process of exchange is the process of life. We inhale oxygen and exhale carbon dioxide. The blood system carries nutrients and oxygen to the cells of the body and carries away waste products of metabolism. The exchange gives life to our bodies.

Exchange takes place through crisis, and crisis is normal to life. Birth, when a baby exchanges the womb for the world, is a crisis. Through the crises of life, maturity increases until death, which is the final crisis. Each step of maturity generally occurs through some crisis. Change produces crisis. *The only constant in maturity is change.*

Each step of growth in a business is accompanied by a crisis: equipment needed, personnel hired, facilities expanded or bought. Change produces crisis, whether small or large, expected or unexpected. The exchange of old for new is usually accepted, though not always welcomed, for the benefit it brings. *Crisis takes you from the transient to the permanent.*

Relationships ripen, deepen, become more intimate through crises. Marriages develop and mature as partners gain greater understanding of each other's needs and desires. More often than not, crisis forces the discussion, they discover each other's attitudes and change occurs.

Death takes many forms: physical, mental, social, economic, emotional or

> Failing is not the worst thing in the world, quitting is.

even spiritual. With the Lord Jesus Christ, physical death was a process of exchange both for our benefit and that of Almighty God, to take us from the transient state of life on earth to a permanent place with Him in Heaven.

Balance. Jesus Christ is God's *communication* to us. Calvary is the place where Christ *exchanged* His righteousness for our sinfulness that we might give up our sinfulness for His righteousness. Jesus made a new *agreement*, or covenant, with God by which we are assured of eternal life. Jesus provides for both repentance and faith, the *balance* of which unlocks Heaven.

POWER OVER DEATH

Through His death and resurrection, Jesus broke the power of the devil who, through sin, had the power of death. Jesus brought freedom to all people who had been living as slaves to the constant dread of death. Consider some propositions concerning death:

First: *To the Christian, death is only a transition from one state of being to another that is higher.* It's the crisis by which we go from a transient to a more permanent state of being. Crisis is normal to life because it is the catalyst for change. Death of any kind is the ultimate crisis in life.

Second: *Death is an enemy only when it occurs outside Christ.* In Christ, death and life are both servants.[3] Death is the necessary intermediary in bringing a greater dimension to life. Death in Christ is only a process of exchange—the terrestrial for the celestial; mortal for immortal; natural for spiritual; corruptible for incorruptible.[4]

> In Christ, death is a servant to bring greater life through resurrection power.

Life is born out of death in the same manner in which success is born out of failure. Jesus taught that He could not give life except through His death at Calvary. The devil tried to deceive Him into compromising by offering Him all the kingdoms of this world if He would only bow down and worship him. After all, Satan's goal has always been to replace God. Jesus refused.[5]

Third: *Any death in Christ must be followed by a resurrection or it is not death in Christ.* The crucifixion is incomplete without the resurrection. He "was delivered up because of our offenses and was raised because of our justification."[6] God did not call believers to live a crucified life but a resurrected life through Jesus Christ. The resurrection took away death's victory.

Fourth: *The resurrection is the ultimate miracle.* If you believe in the resurrection, you can believe for any miracle. Every miracle flows from the same power that manifested the glory of God by raising Christ from the dead.

Fifth: *Jesus established a principle when He said, "He who finds his life will lose it, and he who loses his life for my sake will find it."*[7] He was simply saying that if we are willing to die to self and this present evil world ("filled with lust and rottenness"[8] is how Peter put it), and throw our total dependence upon Him, we shall find life. Everlasting life!

Sixth: *For the Christian, there are many forms of dying to self.* Repentance is a form of self-death. So are intercession and fasting. Virtually any form of self-sacrifice, no matter how small, involves death to self.

Seventh: *Financial death can occur in many ways, but in many countries, it is mitigated by bankruptcy laws.* Such laws are usually a shadow of the substance found in the Old Testament "Year of Jubilee" the Lord established for the economic future of Israel. "Jubilee" was when debts were forgiven, lands were restored and people had an opportunity to start anew.[9] Such forgiveness was symbolic of death and resurrection.

Eighth: *There is death, and there is a "spirit of death."* The spirit of death is akin to symptoms of illness. Symptoms are not always diseases in themselves but often are merely invitations to have the disease. When resisted, denied and rebuked, they have no effect. The "spirit of death" is often just an oppression to submit to death, but when reproved in the Name of Jesus, it cannot claim its prey.

FIVEFOLD TEMPTATIONS

Look at Elijah, the great man of God. He contended with the wicked Jezebel and her prophet-priests who were defiling and deceiving the people. She dominated her husband, seduced her nation and was infuriated that she could not counter Elijah's influence.

Engaged in a contest with her priests, Elijah emerged triumphant, proving that Jehovah was God, but he ran miles from the scene to escape Jezebel's threat to kill him. Later, wearied with his labors, exhausted from the journey, he sat under a juniper tree, commiserating with himself.[10]

In his depression, he asked to die, saying and said, "It is enough; now, O lord, take away my life; for I am not better than my fathers."[11] Therein lies the fivefold temptation that men suffer and in which the spirit of death desires to take hold of men's lives:

(1) Depression
(2) Despair
(3) Inferiority
(4) Resignation
(5) Failure

Death and resurrection go together. The cross and the empty tomb are incomplete without one another.

God didn't let Elijah die but helped him recover. God caused the spirit of death to leave him, then raised him up to pass his mantle to Elisha and exchange his juniper tree for a chariot of fire.

During my lifetime, I have suffered those temptations, watched great men go through the agonizing process and gloried each time renewed vigor and vitality flowed into the life.[12]

Failing is not the worst thing in the world, quitting is.

The Apostle Paul knew the dilemma and frustration of wanting to do right but being unable to do it. "For the good that I will to do, I do not do; but the evil I will not to do, that I practice."[13] He felt trapped and needed out of it. He was powerless. He needed help.

Then, after knowing Christ, he said, "For the law of the Spirit of life in Christ Jesus has made me free from the law of sin and death."[14]

Although Paul had been delivered from his bondage to sin, his past still paraded before him. In his zeal to persecute Christians, he had thrown some into prison and even killed some. Now that he was a believer, he sat in the place of worship with women made widows by his religious hatred and with men who lost their sons through his persecution of Christians. The guilt of his past was a burden too heavy to bear. He compared himself to those judged guilty of premeditated murder.

The punishment at that time for someone convicted of deliberately plotting murder is unusual to us but fit the crime. The victim's body was chained to the guilty person, and wherever the convicted murderer went, he dragged the dead body along. Ostracized by the community, he found it difficult to survive.

Eventually, the weight of the dead body, guilt for the deed, exclusion from society, isolation from normalcy and separation from family and friends killed the condemned person. That's how Paul described his condition, as if chained to his past sin, guilt and shame. They were a weight too heavy to bear, and if not released off him, they would eventually kill him.

Then he found his freedom from the same source that brought him the good news of his salvation—the Lord Jesus Christ. Writing for all the world to know, he said, "Thanks be to God through Jesus Christ my Lord." He was free!

> Just as the sting of death is removed by the resurrection, so the sting of failure is removed by success.

Freed from his chains to the past, he later wrote, "Forgetting those things which are behind and reaching forward to those things which are ahead, I press toward the goal for the prize of the upward call of God in Christ Jesus."[15]

Death to sin set Paul free to live. By dying to the past, he was free to live in the present with a great hope for the future. In Christ, death is a servant to bring greater life through resurrection power.

Dying is never easy. In any form. Consider this carefully:

If you have suffered job loss, divorce, bankruptcy, losing a friend or loved one—when you commit and submit that to Christ, know this—*there will come a resurrection for you!*

Just as the sting of death is removed by the resurrection, so the sting of failure is removed by success.

The greatest evidence of the faith of Jesus was when He trusted the Father to raise Him from the dead. When it came time to die, Christ totally and completely trusted Himself into the Father's hands, believing that God would raise Him from the dead. He had no fear of death because of His faith in the Father.[16]

Faith is similar to wind—you can't see them—only the results of their presence. That's why James wrote, "I will show you my faith by my works."[17] Faith is seen only by its works.

Have faith in God, not in symptoms, signs, symbols or circumstances. The Word of God is your foundation of faith. Experience serves only as a witness to faith's results.

Don't let the past weigh you down!

Don't let a disaster become your grave!

Die to those things, that you might live.

If you have never repented, die to self by admitting wrong. Do it, so God can raise you from death in trespasses and sins. The resurrection life is glorious in its unlimited freedom and expression.

DEATH TO SELF BRINGS RESURRECTION POWER

The real secret of success is not in the living, it's in the dying to self.

Marriage is successful because each partner dies a little to him or herself to make the marriage successful. I've taught around the world that shopping with your wife can be a form of dying to self. It takes a little dying to build a successful marriage.

Most successful businessmen have died through failure before succeeding.

Every minister wants to succeed, so they train in schools that teach doctrine, language and technical aspects of ministry—everything except the one necessary ingredient that makes living glorious and ministry successful. The real secret of successful ministry is in dying to self.

It's true in every aspect of life. Death brings the resurrection.

The resurrection is worth the dying.

Christ died that we might have life and have it more abundantely.[18] Everyone wants the abundant life but not the death that makes it possible. You can't have one without the other.

Death and resurrection go together. The cross and the empty tomb are incomplete without one another.

Now is the time—submit and commit your life to the Lord—repent of sin and receive His resurrection life. That's the power of life.

You will have an entire eternity to enjoy it.

Part 3

Real Sight

6

Life-Changing Values

WHEN GOD CREATED MEN AND WOMEN IN HIS image and moral likeness, He endowed us with five powerful characteristics that enable us to live a Christlike life, thereby bringing some of Heaven to earth. The five characteristics are:

(1) Capacity to know the truth
(2) Ability to recognize moral excellence
(3) Power to exercise our will
(4) Creative power in our words
(5) Right and ability to reproduce

For the Christlike man, these attributes aid in stewarding earth and family, to fulfill God's will, accomplish His purposes and glorify Him. As these God-given abilities bring glory to God, they also bring remarkable blessings to individuals, society and whole cultures. However, most men today neither recognize nor use these God-given endowments to enrich life and bring glory to God on earth, which is evident by the state of nations.

The U.S. is losing its God-given uniqueness. Begun by diverse groups of people seeking religious and economic freedom, the U.S. has lost sight of her God-blessed beginnings. Author John Anderson wrote that America shows remarkable similarities to the pattern that brought down the Israelites Israel during Hosea's time:

(1) Became victims of surrounding culture
(2) Seduced by pagan worship, saw little harm or difference in religious practice

(3) Thought Canaanites had the better life
(4) Lost sense of God's presence and purpose
(5) Embraced "fertility cults"; sexual promiscuity led to a moral breakdown of society
(6) Moral degeneration led to murder[1]

Lower morality leads to higher mortality. Instead of laying down life to ensure greater life, men may take life because life is deemed valueless. In Nazi Germany where a similar breakdown occurred, the Holocaust resulted. America's holocaust is abortion. In nations where genocide occurs, the value of human life is just as negligible.

John Anderson explains our children's plight:

The cry for a father is the cry to be wanted. The 1940s produced the postwar generation, the '50s the silent generation, the '60s the dropout generation, the '70s the rebelling generation, the '80s the self-centered generation, the '90s the "unwanted generation." From abortion to child abuse, from careers to lifestyle, the message we give our children is "We don't want you!" That is, we don't want you unless it is convenient for us! We will allow you to be born at our convenience; and, if you are conceived when it is not convenient, we will destroy you. And, when we have allowed you to be born, we will spend time with you when it is convenient. Our children are learning this message.[2]

You wonder why we have problems with youth all over the world. They're getting the message: "You have no more value than any other commodity in life."

Not only is the value of people being destroyed, but also the value systems which uphold and give worth and dignity to man.

GOD'S MORAL PRINCIPLES

God's Word holds the moral principles upon which a strong and prosperous society rests. The Israelites adhered to

God's precepts and prospered above all nations, but when they set out to be like other nations, by rejecting Jehovah and demanding an earthly king, they withered internally and the whole nation collapsed. Overrun by other nations, demeaned by wicked kings, Israel lost the glory of their God.

Today, moral principles from God's Word still form the only true value system that sustains life and makes societies worthwhile. Rejection of absolutes makes all rules and regulations relative and slanted to the self-interests of the powerful.

As society degenerates, drifting further from God, it allows humanism, materialism and secularism to establish a substitute for God's value system. The change in the value system of a people reflects on the entire society. The U.S. economy reflects values far from the values of Jesus Christ. A survey revealed that America annually spends:

- $2.5 billion on chewing gum
- $12 billion on candy
- $19 billion on lotteries
- $1.7 billion in total giving to 600 Protestant denominations, less than what is spent on Nintendo games[3]

In their analysis of the vast disparity between what people spend on frivolous items and what they give to spread the Gospel, researchers concluded that personal lifestyle is more important than church life. Church members, who have the Gospel by which men are saved from Hell, the most important message ever given to the world, affirm or deny its worth by their support of winning souls for Christ. This economic research suggests American Christians no longer value the Gospel above all else.

The fall of Communism and independence of Eastern bloc countries show the fallacy of atheism. While the former Soviet Union eagerly receives the Bible, the very nation that made it possible—

> Rejection of absolutes makes all rules and regulations relative and slanted to the self-interests of the powerful.

America—is rejecting God's Word and has outlawed the Bible and prayer in public schools.

My grandson has a poster on his wall that reads, "In case of nuclear attack, the ban on prayer in public schools will be temporarily lifted."

Since the injunction against prayer in public schools, U.S. laws have progressively omitted Christianity and moral values from schools. During this time, SAT scores dropped an average of 70 points, premarital sex increased, the dropout rate rose drastically and American school children scored steadily lower in international comparisons.[4]

The American school system has degenerated into armed camps. What was once a school playground has now become a battleground. Barbed-wired fences surround schools and armed guards patrol hallways. Where once love notes exchanged hands, today drugs and weapons are distributed.

Removing God from human life erodes societal mores and distorts personal value systems by which men live. Christians must develop personal value systems based on the Word of God, apart from society's dictates.

CONFUSED VALUES

Many men are confused in their values. Demas, one of Christianity's first converts, renounced his faith in Christ because he "loved this present world."[5] A value held, then discarded, denotes a tragedy out of proportion to its telling.

Esau sold his birthright for a bowl of stew when he came home famished from hunting.[6] Physical sustenance meant more to him than his birthright. Later, after maturing, he desperately wanted the birthright back but could not find a place of repentance.

Men must value the will of God above all else.

Even before God sent Jesus in the form of a man, Moses esteemed "the reproach of Christ greater riches than the treasures of Egypt."[7] He left his place in Pharaoh's house in Egypt and followed God to an uncertain future in the wilderness.

Daniel held his values even at the expense of his life. Knowing the king's decree that anyone praying to God would be sent to the lions' den, Daniel boldly and publicly continued to pray three times a day as he always had. His faith in God held more value than royal threats. When he was thrown into the lions' den, God shut the lions' mouths. Daniel was delivered, his accusers were slain, and the king glorified God.[8] Daniel held his convictions and would not recant his faith, though the king and people preferred he would.

The three differences between preference and conviction are:

(1) People who live by preference can be negotiated out of their preferences. Convictions are nonnegotiable.
(2) People who live by preference weaken under pressure. Convictions grow stronger.
(3) People who live by preference always dislike those who hold convictions.

When the religious leaders of Jesus' day confronted Him and demanded He stop preaching in their synagogues, healing the sick, forgiving sinners, working miracles and feeding the poor, He refused. Jesus wasn't ministering because He preferred it, but out of conviction that brought Him to earth from Heaven. Jesus knew Who He was, why He was there, what God's message was and where He was going.

Jesus lived by His convictions, not men's preferences.

Learn these points in life's value systems.

First: *Some things are more important than life itself.* In the book bearing his name, Daniel, the prophet-statesman, tells of his friends, "the three Hebrew children." Arrogant men, wanting to replace the Hebrews in court, accused and threatened them. They refused to negotiate when confronted with the choice to worship the king or burn in a fiery furnace. Instead, they grew stronger and incurred the wrath of those who lived by preference. Their standing could be better seen when all others were bowing.

The king's threats to hurl them into a furnace seven times hotter than usual held no dismay for them. The fiery furnace held no more dread for them than did the lions' den for Daniel. Their convictions gave God the opportunity "to show Himself strong in [their] behalf."[9] When finally thrown into the furnace, there was a Fourth Man with them as they walked about freely, and when the king called for them, they came out unsinged, without even the smell of smoke on their clothes.[10]

People who live by conviction are considered peculiar by those who live by preference.

Prophets always precede the deliverer. John the Baptist was the forerunner to Jesus. To John, the honor of God was more important than his life. When John angered King Herod's wife Herodias by pointing out her sin, she told her daughter to ask for his head. At a banquet, King Herod displayed on a silver platter the head (and values) of John the Baptist.[11]

Men have dueled and died defending their honor. Women have died under a rapist's attack, fighting for their virtue, which they esteemed more important than their life. On the other hand, perverted values cause addicts to abandon their honor for a few moments of pleasure.

On a far grander scale, Jesus Christ considered our presence in Heaven more important than His own life, dying for us while we were enemies of His, to make it possible for us to become the people God created us to be. His basic motivation was love for the Father, His mission was to seek and save the lost, and His ministry is as our Prophet, Priest and King.

Men who live the Christian life do not count their lives dear. Contending for the faith is not a slogan, nor a motto, but a way of life. Loss of job, money, career and reputation are forms of death to them, but they risk it gladly for the Gospel's sake.

Jesus lived by His convictions, not men's preferences.

Some cautioned Pat Robertson against taking strong public stands on his Christian beliefs, warning him he might lose the entire Christian Broadcasting Network. He replied, "I started with $70, and I've got at least $100 in my pocket now, so I guess I'm ahead." With that, he put in perspective his esteem of the half-billion dollar network he founded. Christ meant more to him than all the achievements, reputation and possessions accumulated during his life. People live and die by their personal value systems.

Second: *The intangible is more important than the tangible.* The internal is more important than the external; the unseen more important than the seen; and the spirit more important than the body.[12]

Wisdom is more valuable than rubies; love superior to sex; respect more substantial than money; a good name more to be chosen than riches;[13] honor more valuable than position.

It is not unusual for men who miss the value God places on human beings to regard people as commodities. Professional athletes struggle with that throughout their careers, feeling, at times, they are something to be owned, bought, sold or traded. They press for more money as a measure of respect. Many owners see players as just another commodity. Lacking respect for them as persons, the owners discard the athletes when their talent diminishes.

One reason for many a woman's negative attitude toward men is the feeling that they find value only in her body, not in her as a person. The prostitute limits her value to the functions her body performs and sells herself according to that value. Her value generally comes to her first by her father, then other men, and finally her pimp. Such women throw away their lives on drugs, because to them, they seem worthless.

A wife often comes to think that her only value to her husband is in service to him. When she begins to think of herself only in servile terms, she loses value in her own estimation. And a husband who views his wife as just another commodity, having no more

People who live by conviction are considered peculiar by those who live by preference.

value than his car, computer or other possessions, tends to show her little respect. Some husbands give more time and attention to their cars than to their wives. When a man's car begins to age, shows signs of wear and tear or no longer serves him as expected, he looks at other models and thinks of a trade-in. Too often he does the same with his wife, which can account for part of the high divorce rate.

Respect is an intangible that is more important than the tangible. Women have accused men of wanting a lady in the living room, a cook in the kitchen and a whore in the bedroom. Respect gives dignity to life. The Lord told the husband to love his wife and the wife to respect her husband, for you cannot submit to someone you do not respect.

I heard the humorous story about the couple who became concerned about his illness. He grew steadily worse, so she took him to doctors who spent all day examining him. When the husband finally appeared, his wife asked how serious the doctor said his condition was. "He didn't say," he said.

"Well, I want to know," she insisted, barging into the doctor's office. "I want to know. Is he going to live or die?"

"Take it easy," the doctor said. "All he needs is three good meals every day, sex twice a day, and he'll be just fine."

She returned to the waiting room and her husband asked, "What did he say?"

"He said you're going to die."

Around my city, we commonly see the "Newport Beach Phenomenon"—older men with younger women. More often than not, the man is some successful professional whose children have left home and whose wife is aging, and he divorces her to take up with a younger woman. His wife may have sacrificed to put him through school, slaved alongside him when he started his business, devoted herself to rearing their children, and now, when she can enjoy the fruit of her labor, he turns her out to fend for herself while he prances around with younger women who satisfy his male ego. *A man must understand that if a woman's loyalty can be bought, then it is no virtue and can be sold again to the highest bidder.*

Later years are those when a ripened marriage can truly be "golden." Today I take more pleasure in my wife Nancy's pleasures than I do in my own. My tunnel vision concerning work leaves me little desire for anything else, so when I travel, I almost never see the sights in the city where I'm going unless Nancy goes with me. Then I enjoy them through her as much as with her. It pleases me to see her pleasure. I enjoy making her happy. I know the value of the woman God allowed me to marry.

Nancy has proven her worth and value over the years of our marriage. I could never catalog all she has done for me—working to support me in the early years, keeping a meticulous house, faithfully stewarding the children through school and the maturing process, moving willingly with me at each new venture, watching the checkbook, forgiving my errors and sins, encouraging me in my failure, standing in the shadows when the spotlight of success fell on me, never missing a day reading the Bible or praying for her family and being the hub around which the wheel of the family turned. Now that she shows signs of her age, needs a little more attention, I should begin to look for a new model? How absolutely asinine! Nancy has *increased* in value over the years. These are my years to give back to her some of what she has poured into my life. It's called *gratitude*. It's an element of love.

Others without a value system given to them from the life of Christ and His Word dishonor God though they may be religious in practice. Of this sort are preachers whose attitude toward their parishioners is that they are just "tithers" and have no real value as persons. Such commercial preachers have existed from time immemorial. "By covetousness they will exploit you with deceptive words," Peter said.[14] The prophet Jeremiah said they "prophesy lies" in

> When a man claims his value system is his own, that he will live and die by it, he becomes his own messiah.

the Lord's Name.[15] Their ways are pernicious, noxious and even fatal. Avoid them!

"The good shepherd gives His life for the sheep."[16] As Christ Himself was willing to do what was necessary for those God loved, so true shepherd-preachers lay down their lives for their flocks. Thank the Lord for godly pastors!

Third: *Money clarifies your values.* Money gives the appearance of worth. The more we pay for something, the greater the respect we show. Cars, homes, antiques, jewelry are given value through the money we spend on them. You get what you pay for. *We tend to invest our money in the things we value the most.*

Many men establish their own worth or value by the esteem in which they hold themselves. Though some may esteem themselves too highly, others not enough, we must recognize our worth in terms of both money and respect.

Working in the warehouse at five dollars per hour and envying the man behind the glass barrier upstairs in his tie, making fifty dollars per hour, will not change your worth. To increase in value, work on yourself. Education is a lifelong process, not just for teen-time. You are never too old to learn, only too lazy to try.

There is an enigma concerning money and the Gospel. Church members admit that their ministers handle the words of eternal life but are content to leave them as nearly the lowest paid of all professions. Pastors are worthy of "double honor."[17] Godly pastors are more valuable than governors or presidents because they watch after your soul's health.

For the first few years of our ministry to men, we subsisted on the free will offerings of meeting attendees. That all changed when a principle of the Kingdom of God sprang to life for me.

Jesus said, "Where your treasure is, there your heart will be also."[18]

Realizing that, when people invest money into something, they are going to be far more interested than mere spectators, we instituted a registration fee for our events. Men now stay for the entire event and attend even when the weather is atrocious. That paid registration fee became a treasure invested, so they put their hearts into the meeting.

That principle also teaches you that you can't build a church with people who don't tithe or invest financially in the church. Without the investment, they don't have their hearts in it. Their affection will follow their profits. If the church is without profit to them, they have no love for it. Duty will not keep them there when adversity comes.

It is easy to be seduced by the culture around us, to embrace its values and to lose sight of the God-called life. The world believes that the Church should be poor and beggarly, without financial stability to advance the cause of Christ and that preachers should minister with a paltry income. To adopt that attitude is to allow the world to set standards for God's work.

Unregenerate men do not value the Church or the Gospel, so why should Christians regard their advice on finances? Without the "birthright" of Jesus Christ, they have no interest in the Church.

Fourth: *Whoever dictates your values becomes your god. Who is your god?*

Your value system is usually created by God, you, or others—corporations, philosophies, religions, prophets or parents.

Corporations dictate employees' value systems by wanting them to serve the corporation above God, family or self. The call to worship the corporate logo with sacrifice is not uncommon today.

False prophets, gurus, vain philosophers and wolves in sheep's clothing, become gods to their followers who worship in slavish devotion. Satan's "messianic complex" is the core of cults and false religions.

Communism, rooted in atheistic anger, became the deity of two generations of people. Marx and Lenin became the prophets of the new religion. But Communism was predicated on a lie, now obvious by its failure and collapse. Meanwhile, the Gospel of Jesus Christ, so hated, ridiculed and denied as the "people's opiate," is being eagerly embraced, not as a narcotic, but as a cure, immunizing them against the toxin of tyranny.

Collective value systems are comprised of those of individuals.

When a man claims his value system is his own, that he will live and die by it, he becomes his own messiah. His counterfeit "trinity" is "me, myself and I." Refusing to accept Christ, the true Messiah, a man comes short of the glory of God and will suffer the consequences for eternity. As his family's messiah, he will answer for his idolatry when he stands before God.

Fifth: *Individual rights cannot exceed the corporate good.* Nowhere is this more obvious than in the human body. The appendix, expending on itself the vitality meant to give life to the entire body, must often be removed for the sake of the health of the body. Allowing one member of the body to usurp the functions of all is deadly.

Around the world, AIDS activists can be anarchists in their insurrection, demanding that moral men pay for the ills of the immoral. Dictators, in their lusts, rape the country to satisfy themselves, making their individual pleasure more important than the prosperity of the people.

Though theologically debated, the Apostle Paul's warning to women not to speak out in church was an application of this very principle. Their exercise of free speech disturbed the meeting, distracted the speaker and put the entire meeting in disarray. Paul's injunction was never meant to be a muzzle on a woman's gifts, just inappropriate utterance.

The value of the whole exceeds the value of the one.

Doctors major in health, not disease. The only reason they diagnose a disease is to find a cure. There is no cure needed without a disease. Surgery of the diseased appendix is necessary for the body to live. "Cutting out" the unsound is sound.

The greatest value of a father's legacy is in the faith he leaves in his child's life.

For the same reason, the Apostle Paul advised the Corinthian church to set aside the immorally incestuous members. "A little leaven leavens the whole lump."[19] By giving the "brother" the benefits of membership in the church, there was no need for repentance of his sin.[20] By excising him, requiring repentance for readmission, the fear of the Lord would bring him to the place of repentance and restoration.

I had a cutback in my staff and never went through such agony before. The decision was difficult, but necessary for the ministry to survive. Cutbacks in business in recessionary times are not because employers don't like employees, but because the survival of the business is at stake, and it has priority over the individual.

Not long ago, a union went on strike against a major corporation and continued the strike until the company went out of business. Then, when the union members lost their jobs, they blamed the corporation. They were insisting on their individual rights—and they got them—the right to do anything they wanted once they lost their jobs. This is not to discount people's desire or need for respect as individuals, nor to give license for immoral men to lord it over employees and treat them as chattel, but to give a principle by which we are to be guided in our values to work for the common good of all.

Sixth: *Fathers provide the family's value system.* Fathers provide the atmosphere in the home, whether the father is present or absent. Children learn theory at school but how to live at home. *A father's responsibility is not to make his son's decisions but to let his son see him make his.*

When I was a boy, my mother faithfully took me to church, but my dad never attended. He loved pleasure, the fellowship of other men, recreation and sports, gambling, drinking, and so I left the church and followed Dad's path. Fortunately, I could not outrun my mother's prayers, so for almost the last half-century, it has been my joy to serve the Lord.

The attack on the family that has increased in intensity in recent years has occupied the attention of ministers, but they have largely failed to correct the condition. The biblical pattern for the discipling of the family is this: *The pastor disciples the man and the man disciples the family.* However, for two generations, pastors have taught men to bring their families to church, and they will take the responsibility to disciple the family, through Sunday School, youth programs, ladies' Bible studies and other assorted activities. In so doing, the pastor becomes the surrogate father to every member of every family who attends the church. That is a burden too heavy for any one man to bear.

The greatest value of a father's legacy is in the faith he leaves in his child's life. His child's greatest treasure is his faith in God. It is of such value that it is invaluable.

Seventh: *Values can be held, then discarded.* Unfortunately, they often are. Consider this tragic example from the New Testament.

Some of the saddest words ever written about any man are those of Paul writing of his former co-laborer, "Demas hath forsaken me, having loved this present world."[21] Failing to esteem the reproach of Christ of greater riches than the pleasures of this world, Demas turned his back on the Gospel and returned to his love of the world.

Did you ever see a dog vomit, then return and eat it? That's how Peter described a man rejecting Christ and returning to his life of pleasure and sin.[22]

In a meeting in Philadelphia, a gentleman who looked as if he were an executive or successful salesman cornered me in the hallway. "I just wanted to tell you what happened to me today. My company gave me my bonus check. It was much larger than I thought it would be, and because it was enough money to buy some 'white powder,' I thought of doing it and celebrating my good fortune. Then I remembered about the dog and the

> Time wasted is lost. Time spent is gone. Time invested is multiplied.

vomit and the taste went out of it. Thanks for showing me that the old things are so putrid."

Don't discard the most valuable gift imaginable, the gift of salvation and friendship with God, for a few moments of ethereal and ephemeral pleasure with those who are wasting their lives. What value is there in that?

Every day, in every way, thank God for the gift of life. Appreciate its value, cause it to increase in your life, and above all else, give praise to the God of Heaven Who considered you valuable enough to pay the price for your eternal life. Your true value is in the value in which God holds you. That's eternal worth.

Eighth: *Everything in life has value.* Actual, perceived, accrued. Some things are taken for granted and their value goes unappreciated until they are lost, stolen or simply gone. One of them is time. Intangible, ill-treated, yet so bad when there is no more. *Time has intrinsic value.*

Time wasted is lost.

Time spent is gone.

Time invested is multiplied.

When money or health diminish, they often can be regained, but not time. Once time has gone, it can be recalled or regained only in memory, not in actuality.

Timing is the essential ingredient in success—being the right man at the right time in the right place. It's possible to be the right man at the right place but not at the right time and fail. Many mediocre men make a great success because they have come to the fore at the right time.

Influence has value. Leaders determine to influence. Followers happen to influence. Using influence is wise. Selling it can be a criminal act. Companies pay advertising firms billions of dollars to influence people for their product.

Every man has influence. How you use it determines its value. Jesus used His influence to call people to God. His influence on people's lives is felt in every corner of the world, and His influence through people benefits society. The influence from the baptism of the Spirit with power is for the benefit of all mankind. The manifestations and gifts of the Spirit are to witness to the Gospel of Jesus Christ. Using them only for personal benefit is immoral.

There is even value in failure. *Yesterday's dung is tomorrow's fertilizer.* One man's junk is another man's antique. What seemed worthless yesterday may have great value tomorrow. Never throw away your failures. Use them as the underpinning for right decisions today and tomorrow.

What is the stigma of Christianity to some is the glory of the cross to others.

The Bible very clearly lays out the value system God has for this world and for us as men. He valued us enough to send Christ to die for us. When we reject that basic truth, we call God a liar.[23] What makes a man think that after spending a lifetime rejecting God's Word, calling God a liar, aligning himself with God's enemies, that when he dies, God is gladly going to receive him into Heaven?

God establishes the value systems for the Church and the individual, and God is no pauper. God's throne and tabernacle in Heaven are without peer. Nothing can compare with His glory. All the majesty of all the royalty that ever existed on earth combined cannot compare with a scintilla of the glory of God.

Eternal values in life are established by God through Jesus Christ.

To become a real man is to have real values.

Maximizing Your Resources

THE SUDAN IN AFRICA IS A LAND UNDER SIEGE. Elements and people have taken their toll. The Sudan had a famine that took the lives of 250,000 people. Civil war had wiped out 500,000 over the previous six years. Many of those annihilated were a tribe of giants called the Dinka, most of whom stand six feet tall and whose chiefs are always over seven feet. The Dinka are a warrior people who place great emphasis and pride on such things as courage and physical stature. Dinka males often bear scars from wounds suffered in spear and club fights. Among the Dinka, theft is almost nonexistent. A Dinka's word is his bond.

When asked by a reporter what it means to be a Dinka, the chief replied, "It means that one must be a husband to all people. It means one must protect others, provide for others, but always be ready to step in and decide what is right and wrong. A Dinka must be strong. He must be a man among men."[1]

Being a man in almost every culture means being ready to direct, protect and correct. The three elements stem from God's instruction to Adam to guide, guard and govern.[2]

Many cultures subject boys to bloody rites of passage. Besides the shedding of blood, almost all include imperviousness to pain, exemplary courage in the face of danger and the unflinching resistance to all threats to his manhood. Tears, softness or weakness disqualify manliness.

> Ministers don't own the ministry they are in. They are only stewards of the grace God has given them.

Anthropologist David Gilmore, in his book, *Manhood in the Making: Cultural Concepts of Masculinity*, wrote:

> In East Africa young boys from cattle-herding tribes ... are taken away from their mothers and subjected to painful circumcision rites by which they become men. If the Samburu boy cries out while his flesh is being cut, if he so much as blinks an eye, he is shamed for life as unworthy of manhood. The Amhara, an Ethiopian tribe, have a passionate belief in masculinity called "wand-nat." To show their "wand-nat," Amhara youths are forced to engage in bloody whipping contests.[3]

Mr. Gilmore cites other bloody ordeals. In Melanesia, young boys are torn from their mothers and forced to undergo whipping, bloodletting and beating, all of which the boys must endure stoically. The boys of the Tewa in New Mexico are taken away and lashed on the back with a crude yucca whip that draws blood and leaves permanent scars. "You are made a man," the elders tell them afterward. The aboriginal Mehinaku of Brazil scorn as effeminate those who are stingy, weak or impotent.

In America, baseball and football are rites of passage. Some fathers consider "making the team" almost a matter of life and death. The intensity with which some dads pressure their sons into emotional stress beyond their years is appalling. These men are not aborigines, just American men, but with the same propensities as tribal leaders, and whose games may not be with sticks and stones but even more lethal modern equipment. Baseball, football and basketball are often violent. There isn't much difference among men after all, just various methods of accomplishing the same maturation process.

Mr. Gilmore stated:

> I've discovered there is almost a generic criterion of manhood across diverse societies. Manhood is based on being competent in three things: The first is provisioning.

A real man provides for his wife, his children and his group ... protection ... Defending your clan or country is exclusively a male duty ... impregnating ... In many cultures, having lots of children and wives or mistresses shows that you're a real man.[4]

"Real men" are those who give more than they take, who ... serve others by being brave and protective ... Real men do nurture. They do this by shedding their blood, their sweat, their semen; by bringing home food, producing children or dying, if necessary, in far away places to provide security for their families. But this masculine nurturing is paradoxical. To be supportive, a man must first be tough in order to ward off enemies; to be generous, he must first be selfish in order to amass goods; to be tender, he must be aggressive enough to court, seduce, "win" a wife.[5]

In his research, he found the commonality among men is to provide their blood, sweat and semen for their progeny. Men are to be givers, surrendering themselves, even to extreme suffering, for the single purpose of providing for their clan, household or family.

But a man (or a woman, for that matter) cannot provide what he does not possess. He can't give his wife a necklace if he doesn't have it—or the means to get it. He can't empathize with his wife or children if he lacks love or compassion. A man must first possess what he desires to give. Otherwise, his desire will go unfulfilled.

STEWARDSHIP

We do not own what we possess. We hold our possessions only for a season. Fame is fleeting. Money comes and goes. Friendships grow and falter. Mates walk beside us but eventually die.

Our possessions are not ours to keep but rather ours to nurture and protect. We're called to be good stewards of what we have, whether it be our minds or bodies, our talents or dreams, our friendships or marriages.

Primitive societies have often understood this truth better than we have, particularly regarding the environment. The great environmental concern in our world today is an effort to rectify the damage done to earth by our poor stewardship of its resources. Around the world, waters are polluted, rain forests are depleted, animals and fish are scarcer, and some so rare, they are an "endangered species" with legally sanctioned protection against further decimation. Many are concerned with the depletion of the ozone layer, citing the earth's warming trend as a warning, and declaring that unless we do something, we face the extinction of man ... all due to modern man's poor stewardship of God's creation.

Why? Because humans are basically selfish. We take and take and take but give little or nothing in return. Humans have been this way since the first sin.

Our stewardship of the environment is akin to rape. We use and abuse it, then throw it away. Owners of factories spewing millions of gallons of sewage into lakes and streams, creating a scourge of diseases, when reprimanded and told to stop, spend millions in legal fees to maintain their right to pollute. We behave worse than animals.

When we care only for food and sex, prey upon one another, wander aimlessly through life, seeking only personal pleasure, live by our instincts, we really do live on an animal level. But even animals don't destroy their habitat as we do. Nor do animals contaminate and pollute mentally, physically and socially as we do. The assessment of man's practices paralleled to that of animals gave birth to theories that man descended from primates. Pastor Joseph Ripley said it best: "God didn't model man from a monkey, but men make monkeys out of themselves."

Sons can inherit ministries, but they cannot inherit God's anointing.

Humanity, God's crowning creation—reduced by sin to the pitiful, pathetic polluters of the atmosphere of earth and soul. How far we have fallen, and how desperately we want to avoid responsibility for our actions. That old adage is still so right: "It takes a man to admit he's wrong."

Christ came to redeem us from the curse of sin in order to raise us from the depths of our depravity, give us a new nature with God's own power to be good stewards, and glorify God on the earth. The miracle of God's grace is that He gives us the power of His Spirit to enable us to live the Christ-life. We are stewards of that grace.[6]

Mankind, through Adam, has the responsibility to steward and lead.[7] Jesus, the last Adam, fulfilled these responsibilities while on earth, where the first Adam had failed. "While I was with them in the world, I kept them in Your name," Jesus said to His Father when He prayed.[8] Jesus was a good steward of the men who were with Him. So was King David with his four hundred men. But not King Saul. He exchanged the men God gave him for those of his choosing, and that was part of his undoing.

The kingdom of God does not run on sentiment, it runs on truth. Even those who maintain the faith, love God, desire to fulfill His calling and keep His commandments can make miserable mistakes in their stewardship. "To whom much is given, from him much will be required."[9]

TRANSITION IN LEADERSHIP

Ministers don't own the ministry they are in. They are only stewards of the grace God has given them. All true Gospel ministry is that of the Lord Jesus Christ, and those called to preach are only stewards of His Gospel. It is His Church, His Truth, His Word, His Spirit, His Commandments, His Blood, His Life. His stewards must be found faithful.[10]

Scripture says, "Better is a poor and wise youth than an old and foolish king who will be admonished no more."[11]

Aging has great benefits, but when men grow old in their position, set in their ways, and the time comes to leave, they may choose to leave peacefully and gracefully or contentiously.

Much of what happens has to do with how they regard their position and power. Being a founder and owner of the company can be deceptive when a person's ego becomes involved. Though he owns the company, he is still only a steward, and a good steward must know when to step down and let another carry on the work, trusting the capabilities of a successor.

In ministry, where God anoints and appoints, leaders must be careful in taking succession into their own hands. A classic illustration is in the life of King David who, though old and feeble, remained king. God removed his kingship upon his death, no sooner. When proud aides or seditious sons sought to overthrow David, God preserved him on the throne of Israel.

After Samuel anointed the boy David to be king, Saul became enraged. He chased David for years, but David never retaliated. He had opportunities to kill Saul and ascend the throne a little ahead of schedule, but he never took them. He waited for God's timing. Though David committed adultery and murder in his lifetime, he was God's anointed king. He showed the king's enemies that *when men seek to take God's place in dealing with His anointed leaders, they put themselves in personal jeopardy.*

The Bible records cases where children inherited fathers' business and blessings but had to learn ability and discernment on their own. In a great computer company, the president turned control of the company over to his son, only to lose hundreds of millions of dollars, and had to demote the son and take charge of the management again. The son did not inherit the father's ability or discernment, just his business.

By God's directive, Abraham's sons inherited his ministry and God's promises to him. A great lesson can be learned from Abraham's descendants, Isaac and Jacob. *They each inherited the ministry of their father, but had to dig the wells as their father had before them.*[12]

"Digging the wells" typifies the need for each son to do the works of his father to obtain the same qualifications for leadership. Each had to undertake his peculiar rite of passage. This was not an earthly proving process they sought; it was a heavenly confirmation. Sons can inherit ministries, but they cannot inherit God's anointing.

Ministries taken over by sons, and others, who lack the father's spirit, expire from the lack of life-giving force given by the Spirit of God.

Businesses suffer from successor sons who cannot carry on the fathers' vision, or because no men were trained to succeed the leader, or by bringing in men from outside who have no concept of the vision, principles or goals of the founder-visionary.

Visionaries who launch their business ventures with few resources or little manpower must stock the store, take care of the books, watch the inventory, do it all—guide, guard and govern. As the business grows, they can hire bookkeepers, supervisors, and eventually devote themselves to just guiding the growth. *Though they may have others do the guarding and governing, they can never give away the authority to guide. Only one man is the visionary, and when he relinquishes his role to unprepared men, the business begins to fail. The visionary is the force behind the vision.*

William Tyler Page wrote "The American's Creed" in 1917:

I believe in the United State of America as a government of the people, by the people, for the people, whose just powers are derived from the consent of the governed.[13]

The founding fathers of our nation did not want the power of government to be in the hands of an established rulership such as the English monarchy America had just thrown off. The right to govern is in the hands of the citizenry, not those in the legislative, executive or judicial branches of government. Legislators were to be those elected from the ranks of the common citizen. Shopowners, teachers, housewives, bankers and all other citizens were to be among those selected. Today too many professional politicians, mostly lawyers, hold office too long and become entrenched in power.

Legislators have power only by the consent of the governed. When voters default, unqualified or evil men hold office. To have the power to vote and not do it is wickedness. In the parable of the talents, Jesus said the servant who did nothing was wicked and slothful, insolent and indolent.

When moral men abandon the voting booth in a fatalistic attitude that says, "It won't do any good anyhow," they are deceived. Those governed by dictatorial fiat but who have regained the right to vote, regard it as almost a sacred duty. Recognizing the responsibility to govern, by voting and monitoring those elected, is being a good steward. *Poor stewardship of the polling place is bad citizenship.*

God gave Adam the charge to guide, guard and govern the earth and its reproductive process. When Eve and a family followed, Adam became a steward of his entire family with the same threefold responsibility, to guide, guard, govern.

This translates into: direct, protect, correct. Nourish, cherish, admonish.[14]

In the triune nature of the Godhead, theologians have given us an understanding of the Father, Son and Holy Spirit:

> Son = the Visionary
> Holy Spirit = the Administrator
> Father = the Ruler

Man, in God's image, has the triune responsibility to be the visionary, administrator, ruler. When Christ came, He revealed Himself as Prophet, Priest and King.

As Christ is to the Church, so a husband is to his wife, his family, his possessions, his job and all else that God has given him. Man's stewardship can never be relinquished. *A man is judged by the degree to which he succeeds as a steward.*

A man's responsibility to his family is to direct, protect and correct; to nourish, cherish and admonish; to be prophet, priest and king. Prophets speak for God to the people. Priests speak for the people to God. Kings are qualified to rule by their willingness to serve. Men are required to fill all three roles. When a man accepts that assignment from God, the family structure falls into place. When he doesn't, the result is a family out of order and even out of control.

A man's family is a reflection of his godly stewardship. It's the reason for God's requirement to assess a man's ability to lead his family as the proof of his ability to lead a church.[15] The family is the microcosm of the Church.

A man may succeed as a steward in business but fail as an agent of God at home. The determination of his success or failure is not in what he takes but in what he gives. *The more he serves, the greater he becomes.*

Jesus came not to be ministered to but to minister. Real men hold that same attitude.

8

Staying on Top

AS I DROVE INTO LOS ANGELES TO MINISTER AT AN inner city church, the area began to look familiar. A street sign caught my attention, and I realized that I had lived there! Redirecting my car, I drove through the neighborhood and saw the house I had lived in as a boy. I began to reflect on how many decades it had been.

Driving home after the meeting, I began to reminisce about my life. I had not thought about some of those events, places or things in years. Boyhood in Los Angeles, the Coast Guard, marrying Nancy, salvation, the pastorate, the mission field. Some of it almost seemed like a former life. My reverie brought me to the present joy and fulfillment I have with a ministry to men and how God's Word had continued to change my life to bring me to this day. I meditated for a moment on the specific words that changed the direction of my ministry and career.

In 1974, Joy Dawson was teaching a series on intercessory prayer at the church we pastored. Joy taught us that prayer produced intimacy. It was her teaching on the "Nine Principles of Intercessions" that changed my marriage to Nancy. *Our prayer time together began to produce vulnerability and affection that changed our marriage.*

Just as Jesus was God's revelation of God on earth, so you stand in Christ's stead as God's revelation to others.

There was more. One beautiful afternoon during her stay, an associate pastor and I escaped to the golf course for a quick nine. Joy wanted to go with us. That afternoon she was an irrepressible free spirit—barefooted, running, skipping, laughing and proving she could still do back flips. Then suddenly, just as I was lining up a putt, she said, "I have a word for you, Ed. You can be one of God's thousands of disappointments or one of His few successes. To succeed, you will need a higher degree of holiness and a far better understanding of intercession." I missed the putt but got the point.

At the sound of her words, there was an immediate awareness that this was divinely inspired. Taking it to heart, Nancy and I accepted the challenge and began to practice the nine steps of intercessory prayer Joy taught. The results were revolutionary.

Years later, the Lord impressed me again with His word. At the time, I was fasting and walking the beach daily in the cool, foggy, predawn hours. As I cried out to God all alone, His Spirit spoke five "words" to my spirit. They were:

"Sanctify yourself."
"Preach the Word."
"Go doubting nothing."
"Use the gold, but don't touch the glory."
"Pray this prayer: Acts 4:29."

Five years later, George Otis attended a dinner meeting where I was enlisting sponsors for a new ministry to men. During his message, he suddenly stated, "This ministry is running late."

I realized this was a statement that I should regard sacredly and obediently. Within twenty-four hours, I resigned the church and every organization I was working with. Forty-eight hours later, from my garage, I launched full-time into a ministry to men.

In late 1979, one morning at home over breakfast, I related the text of my initial message to men to my wife and daughter, commenting on the problem of sex sins in society and the religious community. My daughter Joann asked, "Dad, don't you know sex sins will be the problem of the Church in the eighties?"

On the first weekend of February 1980, at a men's retreat in Oregon, I made that statement. I did not realize how prophetic it was. By the end of the decade, newspaper headlines flaunted the sexual dalliances of ministers and church leaders, and distraught ministers and congregations faced the dilemma of discipline, forgiveness and restoration in grace and love for those involved. The 1980s were called the "Decade of Greed." Greed is a manifestation of lust.

HEARING GOD

That brief history illustrates that God speaks in various ways at various times. For example, He speaks through:

- **His Word.** God speaks to us from His Word, the Bible. That is the rule, not the exception, so daily reading of the Word is vital.[1]
- **An audible voice.** This is a special means by which God communicates with man, such as He did with Moses through a burning bush, Christ's baptism in the Jordan or Saul on the Damascus road. This is the exception, not the rule.[2]
- **Angels.** God sends these messengers with announcements, counsel, warning and exhortations.[3]
- **Dreams.** Dreams accompanied by a specific interpretation provide energy for ministry fulfillment.[4]
- **Visions.** God speaks through visual manifestations, as He did to John on the Island of Patmos, to Peter about ministering to the Gentiles and to Paul about going to Macedonia.[5]
- **Spirit to spirit.** God's Spirit witnesses to man's spirit in saving grace whereby we say, "Abba, Father." To be "led by the Spirit" is an evidence of our sonship to God. Our spirits also bear witness to God's and to each other's.[6]
- **Prophets.** Foundational revelation came through apostles and prophets. We are to take heed to the prophets but beware of the false prophet![7]
- **Godly counsel.** For example, Gamaliel's counsel from the

Lord spared God's people. Solomon recognized the value of others' input, too.[8]

- **Gifts of the Spirit.** First Corinthians 12 lists the gifts of the Spirit, and the book of Acts shows each gift working in believers' lives.

- **Circumstances.** Positive or negative, God can use them to confirm His Word in your life.

- **Desires of the heart.** When we are "born again" and become "new creatures," God gives us a new nature. Old things pass away, and all becomes new. As God transforms our hearts, He places desires and dreams within us that will guide our lives, as He did with Joseph.[9]

These various avenues through which God leads us are a way of life for real men. *If God wants to bring His message to a police station, hospital or construction site and you are there—you become God's revelation to those people.*

Just as Jesus was God's revelation of God on earth, so you stand in Christ's stead as God's revelation to others. What you do when God speaks to you affects you, those around you and hundreds of lives beyond.

Through the years, God in His faithfulness, has continually led Nancy and me. By hearing His voice through those ways in which only God can communicate, our lives slowly changed into what we are today. God's "word" did not stop at our doorsteps but became something greater in life as we continued to submit to Him, and today the men's ministry is reaching men throughout the world.

"He sent His Word and healed them," the Bible says.[10]

The pattern is: *God sends a word, gives it a body, and brings healing to the world.*

- The life of Jesus Christ illustrates the pattern. Jesus came as the "Word," assumed a flesh-and-blood body and brought the healing message of grace and redemption to the world.[11]

- God gave the Gospel message to the disciples, who became the Body of Christ, and brought healing throughout the known world.

Did you notice that all God's work begins with His Word? His Word launched creation and continues to precede His work, even to this day.[12]

- God sent His Word to meet the critical needs of society and bring the Dark Ages to an end. God needed men to know He saved them, not by works, indulgences or priestly pardon, but by grace through faith. Faith, not works, justified them. So God gave the word *justification* to Martin Luther.[13] Those who believed it and followed Luther became "Lutherans," and they brought a healing balm to the world.
- Another need arose, and God gave the word *sanctification* to John Wesley.[14] The people who followed Wesley and his methodical lifestyle became known as "Methodists," and they brought the healing message of sanctification to their generation.
- The word that sparked the Holiness Movement was *separation*.[15]
- The word that came to the Pentecostals was *power*.[16]
- The word that came to the Charismatics was *renewal*.[17]

Each "word" developed a body of believers and brought healing to all who trusted in the Lord.[18] Each revelation was important because it changed the course of Church history, which, in turn, influenced the destiny of generations.

When the institution of marriage overtakes the inspiration of romance, crystallization sets in.

Immediately following the word, the pattern of revelation and the process of crystallization begins. Nothing is wrong with any true word from the Lord, but everything is wrong with the crystallization of it. The degenerative trap of crystallization is what ensnares most people and denominations, and it is often the culprit when marriages and businesses fail.

It is easier to obtain than to maintain. The pattern of revelation and the process of crystallization are: *Revelation—Inspiration—Formalization—Institutionalization—Crystallization—Secularization.*

THE PROCESS OF CRYSTALLIZATION

Revelation. Understanding God's Word always comes by way of revelation. God does not explain Himself; He reveals Himself. In His own Book, He starts out, "In the beginning, God ... ."[19] Revelation becomes alive in the heart and brings light and understanding. Revelation about God Himself brings a fresh flow of spiritual expression, including new patterns of worship and music. New wine is not put in old wineskins.[20]

Inspiration. Inspiration is the result of revelation. Revelation inspires change through the "expulsive power of a new affection." A dead leaf from winter drops off when spring comes and the sap begins to flow through the tree. Likewise, when inspiration rises within us, the fresh affection drives out the old and brings in the new. Old habits drop off, and new habits are formed. Aspirations are heightened, behaviors are created, modified or removed, plans are reformulated, ideals are restated.

Formalization. The changes brought by inspiration are developed, codified and formalized. A desire comes for acceptance from and association with those who have received similar revelation and share common goals and purpose. In the Church, denominations arise with doctrines, tenets of faith and standardization of beliefs to be passed on to the next generation. In relationships, distance is measured by formality, intimacy is measured by informality. The more distant the worshiper to the initial experience, the more formal is his application.

At this critical point of development, men must return to the Lord for fresh revelation. A new "word" will incorporate new inspiration and stave off the degenerative tendency.

Institutionalization. Over time, formalization will evolve into institutionalization. Men begin to go through the motions without emotions. Doctrines and creeds congeal, and desires arise to maintain the status quo. It is here where, if new revelation is not sought and embraced in order to progress, then technical and mechanical procedures set in, and men commit to maintaining the status quo. This is where dull, uninspired life begins, and the political replaces the prophetic.

Crystallization. The result of institutionalization is crystallization. Areas of life outside the formalized structure are truncated. New revelation is not integrated because of a hardened, unresponsive and negative attitude. Prejudice and faultfinding intensifies and the syndrome of cynicism begins. "Crystallites" become stumbling blocks to others.

Secularization. Crystallization leads to secularization. Secularization is the return to what existed before the initial revelation. It's the end of a process that begins so wonderfully and powerfully and winds up so pitiably and miserably.

Look at the marvelous university campuses, established by godly men of faith for the fundamental purpose of educating their youth and preparing them for a life of Christian service. Today, so many of them are secular institutions staffed by mockers, skeptics and antagonists to the Christian faith. *What started with a pattern of revelation ends by the process of crystallization, terminating in secularization.*

Men determine the process of crystallization by rejecting fresh revelation. God is not stagnant. He is constantly revealing Himself in accomplishing the restitution of all things before the second coming of Christ. How pathetic to see men who have crystallized on God! They are critical and hardened in attitudes, ways and habits.

Passion is the sin of youth, pride the sin of middle age and prejudice the sin of old age. Prejudiced and crystallized, having lost the joy of salvation and leaving their first love, these men assuage their guilt by self-justification, which issues in an effort to ridicule the fresh wave of God's Spirit and revelation.

If crystallized men are unwilling to bend or bow, their only hope is to be broken so God can mend them. Better to humble themselves, repent and ask God for fresh revelation, the restoration of His joy and the vitality of true relationship with Him.

It's easy to picture the religious pattern and process in colleges and denominations, but the pattern and process is derived from individuals. It occurs in marriages, families, churches, businesses. Even nations can fall subject to the process of crystallization.

In marriage the process can take this form:

Revelation: "She's the one!" The new life of love within you sparks an awareness of beauty, music and perhaps poetry. You hear birds, smell flowers, rediscover the joy of taking walks.

Inspiration: "Will you marry me?" The feeling of belonging together is overwhelming. In the wake of fresh romance, you forget old affections.

Formalization: "I do." You take the vows, create priorities for your lives and set your course together.

Institutionalization: "You take me for granted." Failing to recapture or renew revelation and inspiration, formalized lives become like machinery grinding along, often with friction, without fresh oil. The oil of discovery, finding something new to appreciate, another gift or grace, is the essence of revelation in marriage. When the institution of marriage overtakes the inspiration of romance, crystallization sets in.

Crystallization: "It's too late for us." Judgmental, faultfinding, unresponsive attitudes toward each other fill the vacuum left by the loss of revelation and inspiration.

Secularization: Divorce.

My advice to men the world over has been to tell their wives every day that they love them. Turn to your wife *today*, look her straight in the eyes and say, "You are God's gift to me, and I love you."

Go on a honeymoon at least once every six months— more often if you have children at home. This can be as simple as a night in a local motel or at a friend's vacated house and leaving the kids with neighbors! Pray for and with your wife. Prayer produces intimacy.

The other day I looked in my closet, and all my clothes were freshly laundered and put away. It occurred to me I had not appreciated that faithful, loving service, but over the years, had begun to take it for granted. That was a revelation. I thanked Nancy, bought her a gift of appreciation and told her how precious she was to do that for me. This provided her with a word of inspiration.

So often it is the little things that we take for granted that are the basis for a fresh word of gratitude and appreciation. See the attraction it inspires when you begin to confess your love. An old marriage can restore youth to the spouses when both walk in fresh inspiration.

My friend Jeff has spent time with me in meetings, traveling and worshiping. His marriage had institutionalized, but he blamed his wife for it. Then he reread my book, *Maximized Manhood,* and realized he had begun to take his wife for granted. After changing his attitude and approach toward his wife and marriage, he told me, "Ed, I began to treat her every day like I was courting her. When I did, I discovered new things about her I liked, and she began to appeal to me in the same way she did when we first met."

Without going back to find fresh revelation of her, Jeff's path was the same as countless others, leading him to crystallization and divorce. Fresh revelation brought new inspiration.

In business, the process can take this form:

Revelation: "I can do it!" An idea springs up to do something better and cheaper than anyone has done before.

Inspiration: "Let's get started." Research, a business plan and investment follow as the new business gets underway.

Formalization: "We did it!" With the moving of the first units and the hiring of employees, patterns and procedures develop. A sales network materializes, and profits begin to come in.

Institutionalization: "We've never done it that way before." New ideas and a fresh approach meet with resistance. Opportunities are not even noticed because of concentration on the routine. The product line stagnates, and sales level off. The company is comfortable in what it has accomplished and doesn't respond to current trends or innovation.

Crystallization: "They'll never do it." Competition arises, utilizing ideas and innovations, but the crystallized company watches with cynicism. Faultfinding brings lawsuits that fight competitors to ensure they cannot take over the market. The company is dying but refuses to acknowledge it.

Secularization: Bankruptcy or a hostile takeover.

Married, in business, employed or simply living—you need fresh revelation. You need to be inspired to greatness.

If you settle for old revelation without ever finding new, your inspiration will stagnate, harden into a rigid form of institutionalization, and you will crystallize. Crystallization can occur mentally, socially, educationally, politically, religiously.

When the Israelites crossed the Jordan River, Joshua piled stones in the middle of the river. When future generations asked, "What do these stones mean?" the parents would tell their sons and daughters how God brought them into the Promised Land, so their young would learn about the presence and power of God.[21] Each new generation would be inspired to seek the same supernatural power in the presence of Jehovah God.

God is a God of perpetuity. He wanted each succeeding generation to experience Him personally and know His grace and power in their lives. But those who crossed the Jordan forgot to tell the younger, and the younger didn't ask. The outcome was lamented in the terse statement: "Another generation arose after them who did not know the Lord."[22]

Cathedrals, churches and universities serve as reminders of a "word"

> You need fresh revelation. You need to be inspired to greatness.

from the Lord, testimonies to His supernatural power in bringing our forebears out of spiritual darkness into light, but many have lost their meaning through crystallization. Denominations and political organizations, especially, have strayed from their founding virtues. As a result, much of our world has changed from God-fearing to God-ignorant.

A Gallup Poll suggested that, while religion was growing in importance in the United States, morality was losing ground. George Gallup said, "The vast majority of us say that religion is important in our lives, but not the *most* important influence." *Surface interest and involvement are high, but deep commitment is low.*

"We venerate the Bible, but do not read it," Gallup said. "Few Christians say they are making a truly earnest effort to follow the example of Jesus Christ," and only twelve percent fall into a category of "highly spiritually committed."[23]

In the zeal of a conversion experience or in the thrill of a spiritual victory, we must not forget to go back to God for fresh revelation. The Israelites had to have fresh manna daily[24] otherwise it would grow stale and lifeless. If we try to satisfy ourselves only with original revelation and do not discover God anew, we eventually deteriorate into mediocrity or worse. When that happens, Bible reading is reduced to quoting songbooks; prayer is modified to sermonizing to God; faith is diminished to presumption.

FAITH OR PRESUMPTION

A fine line exists between faith and presumption. There is a great difference between God doing the work through us and us doing the work through God. Letting God be "the Lord of the work," instead of us doing "the work of the Lord" is how one Christian author put it.[25] Jesus Christ did not give you a backbone. He *is* your backbone.

"Without Me you can do nothing," Jesus said.[26] Powerful claim. Powerful truth.

At the battle of Jericho, the Israelites had moved with faith and power and were victorious. Then, relying on experience to carry them, they went to Ai and were soundly defeated.[27] The problem: In their self-sufficiency, they failed to pray. Forgetting to seek God, they failed to act in faith.

Adam did the same after Eve's temptation. When she offered the fruit, he didn't pray or ask God what to do.[28] The disciples were prayerless in the garden of Gethsemane, so Christ went to the cross alone.[29]

Seeking God for more understanding and knowledge, obtaining His perspective on matters in our lives and finding wisdom and truth concerning the totality of our lives are endeavors of the real man. Being content to quote familiar Scripture is not a sign that new facets of God's character are being discovered and understood.

The Word says, "Eye has not seen, nor ear heard, Nor have entered into the heart of man The things which God has prepared for those who love Him. But God has revealed them to us through His Spirit."[30]

God has revelation for you! *God always meets the contemporary needs of a contemporary society with contemporary means.*

God never tires of revealing Himself to men, nor do real men tire of discovering God.

Part 4

Real Heart

9

The Cornerstone of Character

ON A CHRISTIAN TELEVISION BROADCAST discussing the subject of faithful men, the host asked me point-blank, "What if a faithful man is unfaithful, what then?"

My answer was just as straightforward. *"When a faithful man is unfaithful, he is faithful to repent!"*

We are all flawed. And when we discover perfection, we have a tendency to crucify it. Just ask Jesus about that.

"Commit these to faithful men who will be able to teach others also"[1] is the principle of discipleship. The common error of transposition perverts that to: "Commit to able men who shall be faithful." That perversion is the basis for problems in business, church and marriage. *God commits to character, not talent.*

When a woman marries a man of ability, talent or dynamic personality, then discovers he is unfaithful, it will make her life a hell instead of a heaven. An employer hiring a man based solely on his resume can have his business ruined by the employee's unfaithfulness. It's common for employers, pastors, anyone to be impressed with men of charisma, talent, ability, and to commit some aspect of management or church life to the man. Then they suffer chaos and loss from his unfaithfulness.

Not only does Scripture affirm that God is faithful[2], but it declares that Christ "was faithful to Him who appointed Him, as Moses also was faithful in all His house."[3]

"He who is faithful in a very little thing, is faithful also in much; and he who is dishonest and unjust in a very little thing is dishonest and unjust also in much."[4]

Faithfulness is the cornerstone of character.

DO-NOTHING MEN

Jesus' parables of the "talents" illustrated divine principles of faithfulness in daily life.[5] In the parable, a master gave a different sum to three servants and went away. When he returned, two had invested theirs for greater returns, while one had hidden his in the ground, not even banking it to collect interest. The master gave the poor steward's sum to those who had increased their investments, plus more to reinvest.

In this parable, Jesus taught the "Law of Capital" or the "Law of Increase and Decline." *By use you possess and increase, and by disuse you decline and lose.*

A man with a nineteen-inch bicep, who can lift one hundred pounds off a table with one hand, places his arm in a sling for three months to keep from hurting it, thinking to take the arm out of the sling and lift the same weight. But by not using the arm, his strength declined and he lost the nineteen-inch bicep and his ability to lift. The colloquial way to say it is, *"Use it or lose it."*

The principle works with faith, love, knowledge, money, talent, whatever a person possesses. Learn the piano as a child, fail to continue to practice, and as an adult, the talent is gone. Hide money away, and years later it will have lost much of its purchasing power. A good steward holds on to what he is given and uses or increases it. *The key to increase is investment.*

Look at what happened to the faithful stewards in the parable. Those who invested their talent were entrusted with more.[6] *The reward for being trustworthy is greater trust.*

The steward who buried his sum lost what he had and saw it given to another. He was not a profligate, embezzler or thief. His sin was not in what he did, but in what he did not do. He was penalized because he did nothing. It's the penalty of the negligent. When brought to account, rather than admit his failure, the steward justified himself at his master's expense by charging the master with being cruel, unjust, hard, enriching himself by others' toil, expecting gain where he had not labored, expected to get something for nothing.[7] *Self-justification has been the error of humanity since Adam blamed Eve, and Eve blamed the devil.*

The "do-nothing" steward's attitude was that returning the same sum should be sufficient cause for reward and recompense. The master's reply was that at least out of fear, rather than respect of the master, the steward should have made an investment and not just buried the sum. Calling the steward wicked and slothful, the master removed him from service. Indolence and insolence are often the characteristics of unfaithfulness. Indolence in doing nothing, and insolence in passing the blame to others.

"Do-nothing" men refuse to do anything if they can't do it all, refuse to help if they are not allowed to lead, and will always refuse if they know others involved could do better.

You build character as you would an altar or building. Block upon block, decision upon decision, line upon line, little upon little.

FAITHFUL IN ANOTHER MAN'S

Jesus said, "And if you have not been faithful in what is another man's, who will give you what is your own?"[8]

On the shelf over my desk is a newspaper clipping encased in plastic, bearing the headline: "Entrepreneurs name top 100 young tycoons." Of the top ten entrepreneurs 30 or younger, fourth on the list is Stephen King of Pizza Hut, Cincinnati. Stephen disciplined himself for years to read the Bible daily, reading it through on a yearly basis, and studying and applying its principles. Upon graduation from college, his stepfather asked Stephen to manage a Pizza Hut he owned. Stephen assumed the management of a business that was deep in debt, had low employee morale and was considered a loser. Applying himself to learn and master the business, Stephen set a specific agenda to educate himself, cut costs and turn a profit.

Several years later, after the first business became profitable, another opportunity became available. Stephen approached his stepfather with a recommendation to invest in it, and seven years later, they owned and managed dozens of restaurants. Since then, the successful operation has been sold for a profit.

By taking the principle Christ gave, applying it to his life, becoming "faithful in that which is another man's," Stephen qualified himself to have his own. The teachings of Jesus are not just for Sunday morning ministry texts but are the source of wisdom and life. Men do not realize more out of life because they are "hearers" of the word, and not "doers."[9]

After I taught this biblical principle at a Phoenix men's meeting, one of the men told us all what the truth did for him.

"I am having trouble with my two daughters," he said. "Nothing I can think of would cause their resentments. Today, I realized I also have two stepdaughters, and I have not been as faithful to them as I have to my own. I've been unfaithful to the daughters of another man. Now I know the source of my problem. When I get home, I am going to become a faithful steward of my stepdaughters, and when I do, I know God will restore my relationship to my own."

Another man stood and said, "For nine years I have been working for the same man, but for the last seven, I have wanted my own business. I believe I can run a business better than he does, develop the business better, and could be more successful than he has been. Now, I realize why I don't have my own business. I have not been faithful in this man's business, so I've never qualified myself for my own. When I go back to work, I am going to become the best employee he ever had, see to it the business is profitable, and then I'll be qualified to have my own!"

Think of how men are curtailed, hurt, denied prosperity, increase and higher position, because of their unwillingness to be faithful in that which is another man's. Frustrated, hampered and throttled, they fail to realize the necessity to prove faithful in that which is another man's, in order to qualify to obtain their own desires.

Faithfulness is the cornerstone of character.

Elisha qualified himself to receive Elijah's mantle by adhering to the prin-

ciple of being faithful in that which is another man's. His faithfulness in serving qualified him for the oracle gift in Elijah's prophetic office.[10] Joshua was faithful to Moses and became qualified to lead Israel after Moses' death. It was critical that Joshua constantly and faithfully serve Moses to prove himself able to follow God's commands in leading the nation of Israel.[11] His submission qualified him for the commission.

"Consider the Apostle and the High Priest of our confession, Christ Jesus, who was faithful to Him who appointed Him, as Moses also was faithful in all His house."[12] Scripture is emphatic in referring to Jesus Christ as *the* faithful one.

Jesus was constant, loyal and submitted to the work and will of His heavenly Father. At least three elemental ingredients are exhibited in His faithfulness: constancy, loyalty and submission.

Constancy means steadfast, never varying, continually recurring. Christ was constant in His application to the Father's will. He was loyal and submitted. He showed Himself to be the epitome of the faithful Man.

Loyalty is the state of being firmly attached to someone or something by affection, sympathy, self-interest or commonality. Loyal men are not secret-tellers. Their confidentiality is uncompromising. They are quick to stand for the cause or the person to which they are loyal.

Loyal men do not tell tales. "A talebearer reveals secrets, but he who is of a faithful spirit conceals a matter."[13] World governments experience "leaks" by people who tell in public what they heard in private, which become problems to those who govern. People who "leak," or murmur, are not loyal to their superior's agenda, but to their own.

Loyal church members do not gossip, find fault or murmur against their pastor. Neither do they listen to rumors from known sources of such things. Loyal pastors who hear things in private do not repeat them publicly. A man complained to me he was getting passed over for promotion. Yet he was openly negative about the people he worked for and showed little loyalty. He was fortunate he wasn't fired.

Confidentiality is a virtue of the loyal, just as loyalty is a virtue of the faithful.

Submission is willingly yielding, giving or offering yourself to an authority. Conversely, *sedition* is revolting against authority to which one owes allegiance. *Submission* is God's answer to *sedition.*

SEDITION

Sedition in the Church today is ripping apart congregations, tearing down families and crushing friendships. To remain faithful today, a man must beware of the subtlety of sedition.

Sedition is an act of treason. It is the undermining of constituted authority with an attempt to overthrow it. In the American justice system, sedition can be punishable by death.

Responsible governments around the world have been destroyed by sedition. Great tragedies, untold human suffering and financial debacles are the results of sedition in civic affairs. "Office coups," where chief executive officers are ousted and the seditious in spirit take over, almost always spell the decline or ruin of the company or ministry.

Loss of respect can lead to sedition. The public display of ministerial misdeeds in recent years has caused loss of respect in both the secular and the sacred populations, blasphemy in the secular arena and sedition in the sacred.

Nathan, the prophet, told King David that his adultery with Bathsheba caused blasphemy against the worthy Name of Jehovah. In the second chapter of Romans, we learn that when ministers preach against adultery and then engage in it, or lecture not to covet and then show greed for money, or forbid others to steal and then are found in thievery, it causes blasphemy among unbelievers.

Loss of respect is the number one cause of divorce in marriages and also in the loss of relationship between parishioner and pastor. When loss of respect for the ministry occurs through ministers' offenses or malfeasance, authority in the Church is shaken.

The Bible calls sedition a "work of the flesh." In the list of gross vices such as adultery, murder, witchcraft and idolatry from Galatians, also listed is sedition.[14] Many Christians understand the evils of drunkenness, reveling, fornication and heresy, but little is understood of sedition. Those are not the works of the devil as some suppose, but the works of human nature apart from the control of the Holy Spirit. You can't overcome adultery by "casting out the devil" when adultery is a work of the flesh. Adultery is overcome by "mortifying the members of the flesh,"[15] dying to lustful desires, rendering as dead the old self for which Christ died to resurrect as a "new creation."[16]

Good citizens, family and church members, reject the thought of treason, yet engage in it unknowingly. Sedition is natural to the human heart, a product of the soul of man in its rebellious nature. *Sedition must be dealt with ruthlessly to get it out of the life.*

A seditious act can be as simple as one parent not enforcing the same discipline on the children as the other parent.

Bill describes his three-year-old daughter as "the cutest and most adorable child ever born." When her mother refused her request for a piece of candy, she crawled up into Bill's lap and asked for it with a "cutesy" smile, a kiss and big hug. Bill gave it to her. What he did not realize was that he was acting seditiously against his wife, undermining and overthrowing her authority in the mind of their daughter. Later in life, when his manipulative daughter demands her own way, he will have forgotten that he himself sowed those first seeds in his daughter's life. What a large fire a little kindling can start. What seems so innocuous can become disastrous.

When Tom gave his son permission to have the car for an evening to take his girlfriend on a date, he told him to have the car back home by 10:30. When the son came home at 2:30 a.m., Tom was furious, took the keys and said, "You're grounded for thirty days. Don't ask for the car!" The following week, the son wanted the car, appealed to his mother, and she said "yes." Knowing what her husband had said, but acting in sympathy with the son, she was seditiously eroding her husband's authority and teaching the son to disrespect his father. She thought she was being kind, not realizing that she was committing domestic treason.

Don't think me harsh. These treasonous occurrences produce animosity, antagonism and hardness of heart that lead to anarchy among the children and divorce in the parents. Unrecognized as rebellion, the damage is incalculable.

"Church splits" are more often than not caused by the underlying work of seditious-spirited people trying to overthrow the pastor.

An attitude of submission to one another will stop the spread of sedition. No wonder the Bible says to "submit to God"[17] and "[submit] to one another in the fear of God."[18]

Even the withholding of tithes, hoping to cause financial distress that will cause the pastor to resign, is an act of sedition.

Submission is the solution to sedition.

Absalom rebelled against his father King David. He sat by the entrance to the city, counseling, consoling and conferring with the people, winning their confidence, while whispering to them that, if he were king, he would be different from his father. He stole the hearts of the people, caused them to participate in his seditious uprising, betrayed his father's trust, subverted the throne and wreaked havoc on the country. God would not tolerate Absalom's sedition, and he met an ignoble death.[19]

At a ministers' meeting in New York, I talked about the sin of sedition. When the meeting, ended a man walked up and began to cry as he whispered, "I didn't know."

When he composed himself, he said, "About ten months ago, a brother from a church I used to attend called me and asked if I would work with him in a new church he was starting.

"He had been an associate pastor when I knew him, and we were friends. So I told him I'd come and help. About four months ago, I noticed a change in my daughters, and three months ago, I sensed a rebellious attitude. They had never been like that before. Then, a few weeks ago, my wife began to talk about divorce.

"I was trying to do everything I knew to be a good husband, father, church member, yet my whole life was coming apart. Today, when I heard you talk about sedition, it hit me. The pastor I came to help had started his congregation with a 'split' from the church where he had been an associate. I didn't think much about it, but now I realize that he had a seditious spirit when he left. I put my family in his congregation, they embraced his spirit, and his attitude got into the heart of my family."

After I shared that man's story, another wrote this:

"I write to you because for four long years, I have been searching for an answer. In 1987, I closed the doors of my church because my wife and family could not stand it any longer. After we left, we discovered I had taken over a group of people that had split from another church together with the assistant pastor.

"When I accepted that pastorate, troubles at home broke out. My daughters split up with their husbands, my oldest son had problems with his wife. My life hit an all-time low. I left the church and ministry, feeling like a failure and wondering what had happened.

"Today when you told about the man in New York who suffered from a spirit of sedition in the pastor he joined, I saw myself. I had taken a rebellious people and, rather than my helping them, they almost ruined me. Today I repented, forgave them and the assistant who got me into that mess, prayed with my wife . . . Now I can't wait to minister to the rest of my family. Thank you."

People can engage in sedition when they are not in submission to rightful authority.

Sedition is one of many forms of rebellion. In His parable of the prodigal son, Jesus gave a pattern of societal downfall and restoration: rebellion, ruin, repentance, reconciliation, restoration. The prodigal's rebellion was not outright anarchy but a desire for independence from the father's authority.[20]

Sin, in its basic form, is a denial of God's right of possession. Men who desire independence from God the Father and want to live their lives apart from His will are, in fact, rebels against God, Who created them.

People came to Ezekiel to hear what he had to say, but then paid no attention to it.[21] Their rebellion expressed itself in indifference. Before Jeremiah prophesied, he elicited a promise from those listening that they would submit to whatever they heard as a word from the Lord. But when they heard the word that was counter to their desires, they rejected it.[22] Their rebellion was in the rejection of God's Word.

If you have been indifferent, unfaithful, a rebel, a victim of sedition, engaged in sedition, then in the Name of God, get it out of your life! In the parable of the Prodigal, you can see that repentance is the pivotal point between ruin and reconciliation. Repent! Pray!

When a faithful man has been unfaithful, he is faithful to repent.

Show yourself a faithful man.

Faithful in the little, faithful in another man's, constant, loyal, submissive—Christlike.

10

Nothing but the Truth

A SCUBA DIVER OFF THE COAST OF FLORIDA invested in every bit of paraphernalia his sport offered. During a dive one day, he saw a man swim by in just a bathing suit. Then he swam by again. The diver was amazed. Finally, when the man came around again, the diver took out his underwater slate and wrote, "I paid thousands of dollars to do this, and you're doing it in just a swim suit. How do you do it?" The swimmer read the slate, took the underwater pen and wrote, "I'm drowning, dummy."

That old joke points to a moral: Things aren't always as they seem. Viewing from a limited perspective does not tell the whole story. All our understanding is practical, at best, and only God, Who is completely omniscient, totally understands all that is in the world—and in people.

God is the Creator. Men are discoverers. We discover gold, laws such as gravity or aerodynamics, and truth. Truth is mankind's greatest discovery in life. Just as men work to discover precious metal, so we must labor to discover truth. Wisdom is found only when sought with the same tenacity, fierceness and effort as seeking gold. *Neither truth nor wisdom is found lying on the surface of life's strata.*

We discover Jesus as Truth only through the process of repentance and the exercise of faith. We must work to discover and embrace truth, regardless of the personal cost.

Jesus constantly worked to change the philosophies, mindsets, attitudes and thought patterns of His disciples. So much of what they knew and learned came from sources other than godly understanding of truth. Jesus, the Bible teaches, is Truth. As Truth, it was His basic ministry to teach, represent and reveal truth as it is in the very nature of God. Jesus indicted the religious Pharisees for embracing tradition at the expense of truth and for rejecting truth when they heard it because it was contrary to their personal desires. Jesus praised those who understood truth as He revealed it, especially those truths related to His identity and mission.

Jesus Christ said, "I am the way, the truth, and the life."[1] Truth is the fulcrum for both the way and the life. The "way" is our direction in life, the "truth" is the moral and intellectual basis for life, the "life" is the result of our relationship to Jesus. *The more we base our life on truth, the better will be our way and the greater will be our life.*

Truth in its relational form is any element of knowledge that frees the mind and heart from error and lies. Such as, truth related to a friend that clears a misunderstanding, an assumption that is cleared by understanding, and even truth used as the basis for friendship.

The power of truth is liberating.

Jesus said, "You shall know the truth, and the truth shall make you free."[2] Satan is said to blind men's minds[3] and thus enslave them, but when the truth is seen, they are freed from the power that held them.

VALUE OF TRUTH

Truth is one of life's most valuable commodities, if not the *most* valuable, yet we disregard it in society today. A national American magazine featured an article about the U.S. concerning lying, cheating and stealing. ABC News spent an entire television hour tracing the decline of American morals and the same three characteristics marking national life, also entitled "Lying, Cheating, Stealing: Ethics in Modern American."[4] U.S. legislators pass "truth in advertising" laws because marketers cannot be trusted to be truthful, and even then, law enforcement officers spend millions trying to enforce such statutes.

A new American report on ethics led to this incriminating headline: "Did We Rear a Bunch of 'Moral Mutants'?"

The report's researcher and author foresees in our future "legions of young job applicants claiming degrees they don't have to get jobs they aren't qualified for ... a tooth-and-nail scramble for economic survival, reward and prestige that will trample proper conduct, honesty and altruism." Seventy-five percent of high-school students and 50 percent of college students admit to cheating. In business, 12 to 30 percent of job applications contain "deliberate inaccuracies." The report concluded, "This generation is the price we are paying for our own moral deterioration."[5]

Lest adults cluck their tongues at the young, they are targeted by another researcher who found "a tremendous craving among young people for honesty from adults."

So little reverence for truth exists, that the entire world suffers from the lack. When Isaiah cried, "Truth is fallen in the street,"[6] his society had already begun to collapse.

Dictatorial governments practice "disinformation," lawyers "bend the truth," secretaries "falsify" reports, children tell "white lies," even preachers speak "evangelistically"—often a euphemism for exaggeration or lying.

Communism's foundation was a lie, propagated throughout the world. Even many intellectuals embraced it, saying it was the answer to democracy's ills. Now that we see Communism's true nature with all its evils, poverty and pain, the truth reveals the lie and is setting nations and people free.

Some greedy doctors bring reproach on medicine by pushing the limits of truth and doing needless surgeries just to collect the insurance. Their profession shakes because of it. This is a lamentable condition, but one that seems to find a counterpart in many other professions.

Truth, individually and corporately, is the only absolute that is a foundation for societal stability. The human heart is deceitful and desperately wicked, without natural love for truth, which leaves a void where honesty, integrity and other moral qualities should spring.

> Trust is extended to the limit of truth and no more.

When truth is discovered, its reality brings change. To change the corporate community, the individual must change. When change comes, it elevates the level of life for both the community and the individual.

An automobile parts dealer admitted that he finally understood why he was losing his business. For years, he had told every customer he could deliver their orders, whether or not he could. He was afraid to lose business, so he made promises he couldn't keep and suffered irreparable loss. People couldn't trust him, so they left him. He learned the value of truth. Built on a lie, his business was failing, but converted to truth, it began to succeed.

George is a man who suffered when he told the truth but gained more than he ever lost. Just two weeks out of prison, he came to work for our ministry. Now he tells his story all over the country. Four years ago, when George came to know Christ, following a drug binge that caused him to cry out to God for help, his first thoughts were to do the right thing. Because warrants due to criminal activity were issued for him in several states, he immediately turned himself in to the authorities. He thought because he was dong the right thing and telling the truth, he would find leniency. It was a shock when he received a twenty-year sentence. He couldn't understand why, when he acted honorably for the first time, the authorities treated him as they did. He thought God would have honored his honesty and caused them to let him go free.

God didn't intervene for two and a half years, then, miraculously, those same authorities granted George's release. Now, George can see where the years he served in a series of prisons became his "Bible school." He used that time to study, witness, minister, pray. Sometimes he was mocked for his faith, but it made him into a strong Christian.

Through the experience, he gained firsthand knowledge of prison systems, from the city to the national level. After leading 150 inmates to Christ, George left with a vision of a ministry to men and the knowledge of how to reach them even when behind bars. Today, instead of a hardened, drug-addicted criminal, he is a kind, tenderhearted believer. He and his wife spend their evenings ministering to inmates' families and weekends visiting prisons. He thanks the Lord for the courage to stand for the truth, even though it landed him behind bars. *Truth was both his defense and offense.*

CRISIS IN TRUTH MEANS A CRISIS IN TRUST

Trust is extended to the limit of truth and no more.

We trust what we believe to be true. When we believe nothing is true, we trust nothing. Perception is not necessarily what is true. Perception can be deception.

Today's loss of truth spawned the lack of trust. People who trust less are often alienated from those around them. One columnist purports that we no longer "watch out" for the company we work for and trust it to "watch out" for us.[7] Instead, everyone looks out for number one: self. Stand-up comedienne Lily Tomlin joked, "We're all in this alone."

Trust is the basis of individual character and relationships. Real men are trusted because they are lovers of truth—the whole truth.

A half-truth is a whole lie. Truth mingled with lies and half-truths is no longer truth. Only truth is truth! To trust beyond the truth is to trust in a lie.

God handed down a principle to the Israelites: Don't sow with "mixed seed."[8] God forbade them to mix animals under yoke, linen with wool, their children with neighboring nations. "Keep yourself pure," became the New Testament injunction.[9] We cannot base our lives on God's Word mixed with lies from a decadent society.

Those who teach psychological principles that are straight from the wisdom of God as revealed in His Word are often of great help to humanity. Those who mix humanistic psychology with the truths of God's Word do humanity a disservice. Corrupting the Cross by minimizing Christ's sacrifice brings confusion.

No lie will ever serve the purposes of God.

- Unbelief is the basis of sin.
- Pride is the strength of sin.
- Deceitfulness is the nature of sin.

No lie will ever serve the purposes of God. Nothing built on a lie will stand. Men cannot allow themselves to become so cynical that they no longer recognize truth and assume everyone is telling a lie. Knowledge of the Bible and the guidance of the Holy Spirit are essential to know what is truth and what is not. Lying is an evil work and bears the mark of the author, Satan, who is the father of all lies.[10] All lies lead to death. Liars are no better off.

Of any people who should be trustworthy in community life, it is those who preach the Gospel. Too often, this is not so, which works to the detriment of preachers who are honest.

At one time, our ministry had a radio broadcast called "Maximized Manhood." There came a time when it was financially inadvisable to continue, and we told our listeners for several weeks that we would have to go off the air due to lack of support. Only after we were no longer broadcasting were we deluged with letters. Many thought our very real plea was a ploy to elicit funds and said apologetically, "We didn't believe you." We told the truth, but our listeners didn't believe us. What a sad commentary!

RESPONDING TO TRUTH

Job said, "Just as my mouth can taste good food, so my mind tastes truth when I hear it."[11] Developing a taste for truth creates a love for it.

Look at how King David and King Saul responded to truth. Their responses displayed their different attitudes toward truth and God, which determined their destinies.

David committed adultery with Bathsheba, then ordered her husband Uriah killed.[12] The murder was a cover-up for his transgression of God's commandment and an attempt to justify his relationship with her. Months passed without

David repenting. God finally sent the prophet Nathan to confront him.

Nathan told David about a wealthy man who was trying to take a little lamb from a helpless poor person. Nathan's wise story incensed David. He wanted to know who could do such a thing. Nathan looked David eyeball to eyeball and thundered, "Thou art the man!"[13] Stricken with guilt before God, ashamed before man, David fell on his face in deep repentance. As a lover of truth, when David heard it, he immediately went before God in sackcloth and ashes to seek God's forgiveness.[14]

At an earlier time, a prophet reproved King Saul for a different transgression. He and the prophet Samuel agreed to meet at a certain place for Samuel to offer a sacrifice to God for the people. Saul arrived first and grew impatient. Tired of waiting for Samuel, he offered the sacrifice, something he knew was strictly forbidden by God. When Samuel confronted him for disobeying God's Word, Saul blamed the people for forcing him to sin. Faced with the truth, Saul sought to transfer blame and guilt to others rather than accept responsibility and admit his error. As a result, God removed Saul from the throne and took away his kingdom.[15]

The difference between David and Saul was in their love of the truth. Saul did not love truth. He rejected it when he heard it. David is referred to as a man after God's heart, not because he repented, but because he loved truth.[16] Saul lost his kingdom and died prematurely. David retained his kingdom and became part of the lineage of the King of kings, Jesus, whose Kingdom is eternal. The result of David's sin brought suffering to David and his kingdom, but he remained king until he died in his old age.

Real men are not perfect. We strive for the ideal but live the real. When we sin and face the truth, repentance is the way to rightness before God. When a man—humble, contrite, repentant—is willing to do right after being wrong, God in His mercy forgives, reconciles and restores him to a right relationship.

To hide the sin and ignore the truth is to bring God's Word to reality: "There is nothing concealed that will not be disclosed, or hidden that will not be made known."[17] "Be sure your sin will find you out."[18]

In recent days, respect for a man I've known for many years has reached new dimensions of admiration, appreciation and affection. I'll call him Jerry. When we met, he was in the process of recovering from the public disclosure of his private infidelities and dismissal from his pulpit. As he went through the throes of his agonies, attempting to maintain his marriage, seeking to reconcile his children, and doing it in an attitude of submission to discipline, I could not help but admire his honesty and integrity. His open admission of wrong, sincere desire to make restitution and earnest employment of Bible study brought him back to the pulpit he had thought was lost. The highest form of restoration for a man who has sinned is to be restored to his former place.

A LACK OF TRUTH LEADS TO A LACK OF RESPECT

Dr. James Dobson of "Focus on the Family" attributes loss of respect as the underlying cause of most troubled marriages in America today.[19] When a woman can no longer respect a man because she cannot trust his word, she no longer wants to bear his name.

When a man no longer respects a woman because he cannot trust her, he no longer wants her to share his life.

Years ago, my wife worked at a large laboratory to augment my pastoral salary. We were getting along well, but the emotional distance between us began to grow. I'm not talking about intense arguments, but petty little picky things, unsettling and unnerving. Like barbs under the skin, they were poison to our attitudes.

One Monday morning, I was sitting in the church office with my staff seated around me. Nancy was on her way to work. The staff and I were going over yesterday's blessings during Sunday's service and activities, talking about tomorrow's plans and discussing what we could do to further the growth of the ministry.

At a moment of convivial laughter, the door opened and Nancy looked in. She saw me there with the staff in a very intimate conversation—to which she was not privy—and quickly closed the door. Slowly realizing what it must have meant to her, I jumped up and ran to intercept her, but she was in the car and gone.

That evening when she came home, I tired to mollify her by telling her what was happening. She would have none of it. I had been basking in the glory of "my ministry," accepting the accolades of "my staff," getting my strokes of appreciation and affection—and she had no part in it. Our worlds were getting further apart.

That episode made me realize I had great respect for what I was doing and little for what she was doing for the family. It started long periods of intense thought and prayer on the status of my marriage, ministry and family. Thinking the ministry and marriage could be separated and both be successful, I had believed a lie. As a result, I had become more intimate with my church staff than I was with my own wife and family. Though I had the respect of the congregation, I had lost Nancy's through neglect.

I also had to face the truth that I had encouraged Nancy to augment our income instead of going before the church to ask for a raise. Cowardice on my part, courage on hers, and now I was having to face my character defects and masculine inadequacies.

Jesus told us to go and make things right with others before we could come and offer our gifts upon the altar.[20] It was my responsibility to make right what I had made wrong.

To this day, I wince as I think about those days. That is why I write as I do, to encourage other men to do right, so they won't have to "reinvent the wheel."

Wife and family come before business, ministry or career. God comes

> When a woman can no longer respect a man because she cannot trust his word, she no longer wants to bear his name.

before wife and family. I had it inverted and had to be converted. Conversion is a constant, not only instant, process. Our freedom from wrong believing is dependent upon our discipline to receive truth. Only truth makes us free.[21]

Once I accepted the truth, accepted responsibility for my actions, asked forgiveness of my wife and family, things began to change dramatically. Nancy and I agreed on a specific date when she would stop working in the secular realm, and God honored the date by increasing our income. We took a family vacation and began to live again as God intended—and the ministry never suffered one iota for the time I spent with my family!

TRUTH CARRIES A PRICE TAG

Truth is not cheap. Truth always costs. A man has to die to himself to accept the truth—and find new life through the dying. Calvary was the price God paid to give us Truth. As Christ died to make it possible for us to receive truth, we have to die to self to receive it. "Buy the truth and do not sell it," the Bible says.[22]

Hold onto truth, not as your possession, but as your Savior and Master and Defender. Truth is your shield and strength. Truth is part of the "armor of God" to help us combat the "father of lies." Only truth can defeat a lie. Truth is our defense, and truth is our offense in all our battles.

Truth is its own defense, and truth is eternal. Men tried to kill Truth by crucifixion, but Truth rose again the third day, and *Truth lives!*

We live to the degree we abide in the Spirit of Truth.

Those who desire to become real men love truth.

11

Love or Lust

FOR THE NOMINATION OF JUDGE CLARENCE Thomas to the United State Supreme Court, the nomination proceedings investigated a sexual harassment charge. Interrogation of the judge and a woman accuser received worldwide media exposure. Anita Hill charged Judge Thomas with making obscene, lascivious remarks to her and intimating his desire to have sex with her. He categorically denied any such remarks or suggestions. He was confirmed to sit on the highest court in the land but was almost barred because of Anita Hill's charges.

Newspapers that same week reported the tragic story of a minister apprehended by police in the company of a prostitute. *At the root of all this is a thing called lust!*

- Pornographers have filed suit against those who are opposed to their publications.
- Pro-abortionists, advocating a liberal attitude toward sexual promiscuity, flail verbally and physically at pro-life advocates who are opposed to immorality.
- Dictators throughout the world use people for personal advantage without thought to the carnage or conflict created.
- The "decade of greed" in America produced a recession, bankruptcies, banking crises and a crippled government.
- Serial killers (both homosexual and heterosexual), rapists and child molesters daily grab headlines of our newspapers.

Wherever you look, you see the decadence, devastation and debacles that lust has produced in human life. Yet, Christians often consider it improper to talk of lust's nature and consequences in open terms. Christianity is based on confession, not suppression. On the other hand, some people accuse Christians of talking about it too much.

Both extremes are absurd. All of us, whether or not we admit it, deal with lust every day. It may be something we see in ourselves, in others or in society. But we know lust is active in our world.

Jesus knew lust's source, nature, causes, consequences. He knew it far better than Freud, who equated lust and love. Freud desired to rid society of the Christian ethic of celibacy and morality and sought to excuse men from guilt caused by "religion." Jesus suffered for those who were controlled and motivated by lust. God and His Word have the final word.

LUST IS PERVERTED LOVE

Jesus unveiled and taught the principle of the love of God: "God so loved the world that He gave His only begotten Son, that whoever believes in Him should not perish but have everlasting life."[1]

Love is the desire to benefit others even at the expense of self because love desires to give. The moral opposite of love, though, is lust. *Lust is the desire to benefit self at the expense of others because lust desires to get.*

Any moral person knows the power of lust's temptation, the battle that rages to do or have something that brings immediate pleasure but negative long-term consequences.

The temptation to sin never comes parading the consequences of sin, but rather heralds the promise of the moment's pleasure. The great deception and seduction of sin is possible because temptation shows only immediate gratification. Blinded by the elation and ecstasy of the moment, everything else is erased from the mind. Only after realizing the moment's folly, and the price it will extract, does the awful reality of the consequences begin to set in.

The Bible says there is pleasure in sin.[2] Drunkenness, adultery, incest, drug abuse, embezzlement, rape, lying, stealing can bring pleasure, but such illicit delight lasts for only a season. When the season is over, their pleasure turns to heartache and hardship.

Lustful desires in the lives of men who want to do right can be tormenting. Torn between right and wrong, pressured by conflicting passions, suffering in spirit, troubled in mind, confused in emotions, struggling to be free, the torment can be terrible. So terrible, in fact, that the thought of giving in and enjoying the momentary thrill can seem too attractive to pass up.

Temptation can be tormenting, but remember: The torment of the temptation to sin is nothing to compare with the torment of the consequences of sin.

Remorse and regret cannot compensate for sin. Many times, my daughter Lois, a prosecuting attorney, has told me of the tears, suffering and pain of people tried for manslaughter caused by driving drunk. Many times, I have counseled the adulterer who wishes to turn back the clock and regain the respect, trust and love of his family. Although they wish they could do it over, no amount of anguish or apology can change what happened.

Though sin can be forgiven immediately, the consequences can last a lifetime.

The first chapter of Romans describes the condition of men "burning" in their lusts. That "burning" is an emotional desire so strong, it overcomes all logic and reason, consumes sanity by fires of passion, and causes seemingly uncontrollable actions.

When a man allows this burning to consume him, the consequent perversion allows him to justify any action, thought or desire. He rationalizes away guilt and condemnation, denies their reality, even blames others for their existence. The Sodomites of biblical days fell prey to this. Through the

> The torment of the temptation to sin is nothing to compare with the torment of the consequences of sin.

deceitfulness of their sin, they became conscienceless, engaging in any form of iniquity and applauding without guilt those who invented new forms of evil.[3] They considered it to be an exercise of their free will, insisting on their individual rights at the expense of the corporate good.

The new "illness" of sexual addiction, amply written about in periodicals and books, is this uncontrolled lust recorded in ancient days. Today, incredible numbers of people have sexual appetites that interfere with the rest of their lives. Literature on the subject lists warning signs of sexual addiction: sexual thoughts that interfere with work and family; spending more money than is available to feed sexual desires; curtailing important relationships because of uncontrollable sexual behaviors; using sex as an escape; and risking AIDS or other diseases just to have sexual activity.[4]

The pleasures of sin exist. We cannot deny them. But we also dare not deny what follows: a voracious appetite, inflamed with eroticism, demanding more indulgence more often until a degenerative spiral captures the soul and drags us on a never-ceasing descent into deeper patterns of immorality and illicit behavior.

Lust goes beyond the sexual. Lust can show itself in a variety of forms: covetousness, gluttony, drunkenness, power hunger and unbridled ambition. *But lust in any form knows no peace.*

Peace can come only through the "Prince of Peace," the Lord Jesus Christ, through the power of His Spirit.

TEMPTATIONS OF LUST

You can torment the tempter by overcoming temptation. There is torment for the godly in the presence of the unclean, and torment for uncleanness and lust in the present of the godly.

Jesus confronted an unclean spirit in the synagogue, and it cried out, saying, "Let us alone! What have we to do with You, Jesus of Nazareth? Did You come to destroy us?"[5] A legion of demons in another man cried out, "Have You come here to torment us before the time?"[6]

The unclean are discomfited in the company of the clean, and the clean are uncomfortable in the presence of the unclean. A vast chasm exists between Heaven and Hell, and a vast disparity exists between the righteous and unrighteous. "An unjust man is an abomination to the righteous, and he who is upright in the way is an abomination to the wicked."[7]

Jesus overcame all temptations. Jesus faced and overcame what the first Adam succumbed to and made it possible for all men to overcome temptation through the power of His Spirit indwelling them. Jesus forever changed the nature of temptation from an occasion of defeat to an opportunity for victory.

Jesus never dealt with peripheral issues but with basic issues of life and death. Jesus met the tempter (Satan) and his temptations in three basic forms. By dealing with temptations at their basic level, He showed His overcoming power over all temptations. On the mountain, Jesus was tempted to turn stone to bread because He was hungry, to throw Himself off the pinnacle of the Temple, and bow to Satan in order to gain the kingdoms of the world to prove His power.

Two of these three temptations stem from lust. The Bible says, "All that is in the world, the lust of the flesh, and the lust of the eyes, and the pride of life, is not of the Father, but is of the world."[8] Jesus fought these basic temptations.

An Old Testament parallel is found in the temptation of Eve in Eden. Eve saw that the tree was "good for food, that it was pleasant to the eyes, and a tree desirable to make one wise."[9] She was confronted by all three basic temptations at once. She took the fruit, shared it with Adam, and humanity has lived with the consequences of their sin ever since.

LUST OF THE FLESH

You don't get to Heaven based on what you know but Who you know. Knowing about church, the Bible and Jesus is not the same as knowing God. When we come to know God and place faith in Him through Jesus, we receive eternal life.[10]

"It's not what you know, but who you know" is the old adage predicated on that truth of the Gospel. People often pervert this through selfishness and use people for personal advantage. Things are *loved* and people *used* to acquire fame, fortune, power or pleasure.

In sexual matters, lust causes men to use women as sex objects. This attitude reduces men to predators and women to prey. It creates abnormal thought patterns, causes mental confusion and perverts the normal reasoning process by desensitizing the conscience.

Pornography, which has been a plague in the lives of so many men, is a financially viable industry because it panders to the basest emotions. And many men obviously enjoy the titillation.

More men subscribe to pornographic magazines than to sports magazines. Even in non-pornographic magazines, and especially in advertising, women are treated as sex objects more often than as human beings, much less joint-heirs of God's blessing.

"The lamp of the body is the eye. Therefore, when your eye is good, your whole body also is full of light," Jesus taught.[11] A pure eye lets sunshine into your soul. A lustful eye shuts out light and plunges the soul into darkness. "To the pure all things are pure but to those who are defiled and unbelieving nothing is pure."[12]

Men corrupted and contaminated by lust see nothing pure in others, either in motive or in deed. They ascribe to others a perspective colored by their polluted minds.

Before his execution, Ted Bundy attributed the atrocities of his multiple murders to pornography. A pornographer's fantasy life, incapable of existing in normal behavior, produces an unrealistic approach to life. For Bundy, it resulted in illusions of the mind that never found gratification, even in murder.[13]

A minister in Dallas pleaded guilty to five counts of aggravated sexual assault and received ten concurrent life terms in prison. He said he started watching pornographic films with the football team in college and never stopped, and he watched them just before committing his rapes.[14]

The Department of Justice reported that during a thirty year period, from 1954 to 1984, in America's three best-selling, sexually explicit magazines, twenty-nine percent of the images depicted children nude and twenty percent related to genital activity. "Almost all" depictions of child sexual abuse portrayed the child as unharmed or benefited by the activity.[15]

A "happily married father of three" watched a "peep show" of a rape three times. Believing that a little girl would enjoy it, he did the same thing to a nine year old. Only "it didn't go that way," he said afterward. "I just wanted to die, crawl up in a hole and die, but it didn't stop there. I still wanted to see more movies."[16] His lusts were virtually insatiable, devastating innocent little girls while leading him to ruin.

The world before the flood degenerated until "the Lord saw that the wickedness of man was great in the earth, and that every intent of the thoughts of his heart was only evil continually."[17] God's judgment was swift and sure. A flood wiped them out. Destruction also came upon Sodom. Fire rained from heaven and obliterated them without leaving so much as a trace.[18] So it could be with our present world unless men turn to God and righteousness.

LUST OF THE EYES

This form of lust is basic covetousness. Covetousness is idolatry because it is basically the worship of self. The counterfeit trinity is "me, myself and I." Self-pleasing is the pleasure principle upon which natural life rests. *Pleasing God is the pleasure principle upon which godly life rests.*

Lust's covetousness can cripple an entire society. In the 1980s in America, sin was consummated on the highest levels of society from the lust that was conceived on the lowest levels of society in the rebellious 1960s. Its voice was found in characters such "Gordon Gekko" from the film *Wall Street*, who said, "Greed is good." Junk bonds, leveraged buy-outs, "greenmail," savings and loan fraud, bribes, all stemmed from lustful men who cared little or nothing about the financial burden they created. The common citizen pays a high penalty for lustful men who achieve power in government or economics—men unbalanced in their avariciousness and consumed with their personal gain at the expense of others.

All dictators are lustful. Ceausescu in Romania wasted extravagantly on his family while keeping the citizenry in nineteenth-century poverty and crusading to eliminate every vestige of Christ from his country. How ironic that a man so filed with an anti-Christ attitude would be assassinated on Christmas Day.

Yet his viciousness against Christ competes with some in America, the "Christian nation." Some claim that Christianity is a threat to society because it does not hold an "enlightened view." This view includes what one U.S. Surgeon General urged, that sex education "must include information on heterosexual and homosexual relations." [19] The philosophy is that Christianity needs to be excised from the national conscience.

RIGHTEOUSNESS IS GOOD

What is "pleasant to the eyes" is not always good. Eve saw what was "pleasant to the eyes" and denied God's command. She chose what she judged to be good only to discover it was evil. In God's economy, only what is righteous is good.

If it is not righteous, it is unrighteous and, therefore, evil, no matter how we label it.

A Jewish doctor wrote a sensitive article, "Why I Quit Doing Abortions." He told how he performed abortions out of a compassionate desire to help women in turmoil. But soon he began doubting himself, hated going to work and his religious practices no longer gave him a sense of well-being. One day a married couple decided to have the baby when the abortion could not be performed due to a medical technicality. Playing with that couple's child years later struck the doctor's heart with the final blow. Had it not been for a technicality, he would have killed little Jeffrey, dismembering him "limb by limb."[20] Misguided compassion can kill. Only God can tell us what is truly "good."

The fear of the Lord is the restraint from doing evil. To remove the restraints, society now advocates sanctions against Christianity, virtually trying to dismiss God from our presence. To remove moral barriers in order to rid society of guilt is a form of civil suicide.

Planned Parenthood is a national organization founded by an admitted amoral social revolutionary devoted to the overthrow of moral restraint. In his book *Grand Illusions*, George Grant tells what Margaret Sanger, founder of Planned Parenthood, wrote in her first newspaper, *The Woman Rebel*:

> Birth control appeals to the advanced radical because it is calculated to undermine the authority of the Christian Churches. I look forward to seeing humanity free someday of the tyranny of Christianity no less than capitalism.

The organization she founded is still trying to break down moral barriers built by godly principles.[21]

LOVE, THE ANSWER TO LUST

The answer to lust is love. Lust is degenerative, love is regenerative.

When Jesus rebuked the hardened-of-heart religious practitioners of His day, He told them, "Ye are of your father the devil, and the lusts of your father ye will do."[22] Satan is the progenitor of lust. It began when he first lusted after God's throne, and he has never stopped. He still desires to be worshiped, which is the root of many cults, false religions and perverted philosophies.

Men accused Jesus of having a devil and being unfair in His denunciation of them. He answered, "I do not have a demon; but I honor My Father, and you dishonor Me."[23]

Lustful men dishonored the Lord by their accusations against Him and cried for His crucifixion because His holiness was a personal rebuke to their way of life. To rid themselves of guilt, they decided to rid themselves of God.

Men carried away by lust are vicious, malicious and murderous in their hatred of God. According to the Bible, they are heartless, faithless and merciless in their pursuit of personal pleasure at the expense of what is righteous.[24]

Lust is insatiable; love is easily satisfied. A man who loves his wife finds her easily satisfying, while a man who lusts for his wife never finds satisfaction from her, despite how hard she tries. No matter how she cares for him, submits her body to him, takes care of the children, pays the bills, works at a job, she will never quench his lustful thirst. Why? Because lust is self-centered, while love is other-centered.

Lust appeals to our greed, while love appeals to grace. Greed can never be satisfied; it always wants more. Grace finds satisfaction in the restoration and happiness of others. Once that is achieved, even if it comes in stages, grace finds satisfaction. Blessed is the wife who is lavished with grace rather than lashed by lust.

OVERCOMING LUST THROUGH THE HOLY SPIRIT

Lust comes easier than love. Because we are fallen creatures, our natural propensity is to satisfy ourselves rather than reach out to others. Even when we are born again, the lusts of the old nature wars against the members of the body, wanting them to do what they formerly enjoyed.

Scripture enjoins men to "walk in the Spirit, and you shall not fulfill the lust of the flesh."[25]

"Put off, concerning your former conduct, the old man which grows corrupt according to the deceitful lusts, and be renewed in the spirit of your mind."[26] Renewing the mind means putting away lustful thoughts and conscientiously engaging in righteous thinking. The renewing process is to fill the mind with the Word and pray for the Holy Spirit's work of purging our lustful desires.

God charges real men today who have the Spirit of Christ to walk in the Spirit and not in the flesh, so they can be "more than conquerors," overcoming temptation and sin.[27] James wrote, "Count it all joy when you fall into various trials."[28] When we are confronted by temptations and defeat them by not yielding, the work of Christ in us is perfected, which brings glory to God.

Job fought a battle with lust and came to an understanding of the only way to rise above it: "I have made a covenant with my eyes; Why then should I look upon a young woman?"[29] A covenant is a powerful tool in the mind and heart of men. Job's covenant with God was a tool that helped maintain his integrity before God.

"For the grace of God that brings salvation has appeared to all men. It teaches us to say 'No' to ungodliness and worldly passions, and to live self-controlled, upright and godly lives in this present age."[30] If this were impossible, God would be in error to command it.

The pleasure of knowing you are a real man before God the Father is greater than any moment's pleasure this earthly world can give you.

Part 5

Real Accomplishments

12

Royal Pursuits

HEAVEN IS PART OF THE KINGDOM OF GOD. THE most heavenly part of living is not the weather or circumstances but the degree to which we bring Heaven to earth in our day-to-day living.

There are two moral or spiritual kingdoms in the world. The first is the Kingdom of God, the other is the kingdom of Satan. The Kingdom of God embraces everything over which God rules and reigns. The other exists as a result of Satan's anarchy against God.

The kingdom of Satan is antagonistic and antithetic to the Kingdom of God. Satan's purpose is still to take the place of God. Sedition began in Heaven when Satan, called Lucifer, no longer wanted to lead worship but to be worshiped. Lifted up with pride, he led a seditious assault on God and was expelled from Heaven, wherein God created a place called Hell.

Hell was originally created for Satan and the angels who fell with him, but when Satan usurped the place of God in man's life in Eden, it was enlarged to receive all who follow his pernicious pattern. Since the first man Adam lost his place with God, it behooved God to send another Adam to redeem human beings and restore them to the place God originally intended, to be part of His family forever.

Every man lives in one of the two kingdoms.

We are born into the Kingdom of God by being born of God's Spirit. We enter into His Kingdom and are able to "see" the Kingdom of God.[1] "Seeing" and understanding carry the same connotation. We can see, or understand, that in the Kingdom of God, everything is positive, while in the kingdom of Satan, everything is negative. Between the two is constant tension.

God originally created human beings in the positive state of holiness and enjoyed fellowship with Adam and Eve. But when sin entered, the very nature of man was changed from positive to negative and the fellowship was broken.

To restore man to the positive and restore fellowship, God sent Christ into the world to reconcile men to Himself. When a man is translated into the Kingdom of God from out of darkness through repentance and faith, he regains fellowship with God and enters into a positive relationship with Him.

The characteristics of the kingdom emanate from the king, so all the characteristics in the Kingdom of God are positive. All the characteristics in Satan's kingdom are negative.

Light vs. darkness.

Truth vs. lies.

Love vs. lust.

Righteousness vs. sin.

Each facet of the nature of God is revealed by characteristics in His Kingdom. Each is seen in the negative in the opposite kingdom.

God is the Creator, Satan is the counterfeiter. Satan counterfeits everything God creates. For example, the corner barroom is a counterfeit church where the bartender is the pastor, people go there to find fellowship, receive counsel, and be filled with spirits. That's a counterfeit church!

There are two moral or spiritual kingdoms in the world. The first is the Kingdom of God, the other is the kingdom of Satan.

All principles originate in the Kingdom of God. No principles exist in Satan's kingdom, for he adheres to none. *Perversions* of principles come from Satan's domain. For example, there is a principle that prayer produces intimacy. One of Satan's perversions is to promise intimacy through pornography rather than through prayer. Pornography promises the benefits, physical closeness and good feelings of intimacy but results in distance, addiction, impotence and alienation.

Virtue flows from God's Kingdom, but the root of all sin is in the kingdom of Satan. *All sin promises to please and serve but only intends to enslave and dominate.*

God's Kingdom is moral, Satan's immoral. For this reason, men have never found a solution to man's immorality by natural means. "Seek first the kingdom of God and His righteousness, and all these things shall be added to you."[2] Men seek what seems important in life, not realizing if they seek first the Kingdom of God, things in the natural will follow.

MINISTRY AND MONEY

Money follows ministry.

When men seek money before ministry, they will not accomplish much. Ministry and money are both means of support.

Money has no morality. It is amoral. Money's only morality or immorality is in the heart of the holder. We give money its morality by how we use it or immorality by how we abuse it.

To have money, men must first minister.

We are prone to think that ministry is just standing in a pulpit preaching, but the truth is, everything we do in serving is ministry. Cleaning a toilet is ministry. Selling a car is ministry. When you wire a house, repair broken pipes, turn a lathe, write a letter, you are ministering. The Bible says, "And whatever you do, do it heartily, as to the Lord."[3] When that Scripture motivates us, everything we do, from running a jackhammer to changing a diaper, has significance beyond the merely temporal.

Whatever a man does, when he serves as "unto the Lord," the Lord

God's plan is just two steps. First, be converted from the negative to the positive. Second, meditate on His Word and adhere to it.

compensates. Many people believe when they are financially destitute or needy, that somehow someone somewhere will appear to take care of them. That is "magical thinking."

Others believe they must have money with which to start a business. That also is a fallacy.

The Bible says if we do not work, we do not deserve to eat.[4] When you are out of work and need money, go out and minister, and money will follow. Examples surround you of men who saw a need, ministered to that need, and ended up building a successful business. When you want to start something new, don't think you can't because you don't have huge capital reserves.

Start where you are, not where you want to be. "For who has despised the day of small things?"[5]

FAITH AND FACTS

Facts follow faith.

Faith determines what the facts will be. The bookkeeper substantiates with facts what the executive did by faith. The fact of the profit and loss statement is not possible until something is done by faith. It takes faith to launch a business, to try a new marketing strategy, to secure a contract for a big job. Faith precedes, facts follow.

PRAYER AND PRODUCTION

The physical reciprocal to prayer is production.

When a man brings his prayers to bear upon his production, he can expect greater results. If he thinks all he has to do is pray and forget production, he fails. Jesus is concerned about production, not just prayer. He said, in effect, "If it doesn't produce, lop it off."[6]

When a man becomes so spiritual that he ceases to be productive, he can become "so heavenly minded that he is no earthly good." He constantly must reckon with both kingdoms. Prayer in the morning preceding the day's work augurs well for the day.

Some years ago, it was my privilege to be associated with a Christian broadcasting ministry. When it first started, the people who were attracted to it were people with a heart for God but with very little expertise in the media, either technically or theoretically. They were spiritual, prayerful, good people, full of faith and eager to volunteer. As the venture grew, the ministry needed to have skills and production, not just the ability to pray. The danger was that as they grew, they didn't exchange the prayerful for the productive. Balance was needed.

Interestingly enough, when the "only prayerful" were replaced by those who were more balanced, the leader was criticized by those who were supposed to be such paragons of prayer.

When profits are needed, a roomful of volunteers is wonderful, but even those must produce. A friend said, after recovering from thirty months on the verge of bankruptcy, "Money is not the most important thing in the world, but when you need money—it *is* the most important thing!"

Prayer precedes production, but production is the evidence of prayer. A praying man who produces is far more valuable than one who has either but not both of those qualities. "Praying producers" are always in demand.

SPIRITUAL AND PROFESSIONAL

Professionals who are prayerful *and* productive are indispensable.

Out of a zeal to please God, men can, to their own hurt, get wrapped up in what they believe is the spiritual part of life. A friend of mine is in distress today because he would not stop witnessing on the job when his boss asked him to tone it down a little. His boss didn't violate his faith or command him to stop, he just said not to take so much company time to witness. Loss of production caused loss of respect.

We want greater results, not lesser. In God's Kingdom, you are concerned about the spiritual—ministry, faith, prayer and things that are eternal. At work, you are concerned about making a living, building a reputation, seeing a good profit. You can feel torn between the two until you have sought God in the spiritual, followed it with the professional and found the balance between them. Balance is the key to life.

When trying to find your balance, establish your priorities first. Seeking first the Kingdom of God causes things of this life to follow. Money, facts, production, professional are all in the temporal realm, while ministry, faith, prayer, spirituality are all in the eternal.

Seeking first the eternal causes the temporal to follow.

Seeking first the temporal misses the eternal. The eternal is always more important than the temporal.

ORGANISMS AND ORGANIZATIONS

God creates organisms, the world creates organizations. Organisms do not deal with "political expediency," organizations do. Political expediency is the attempt to keep everything at peace through compromise. To their own hurt, committee members often seek to avoid personal responsibility.

Most organizations deal in political expediency, work by committee, make decisions based on compromise, avoid accountability and attempt to satisfy everyone. God's organisms, however, deal with the singular, operate through a visionary, make decisions based on principle, accept accountability and attempt to please God.

**Money has no morality. It is amoral.
Money's only morality or immorality is in the heart of the holder.**

God did not create the Church as an organization but as the Body of Christ, an organism. In that Body, God doesn't call a committee to lead a local church by compromise, but a visionary, to whom the Lord adds those needed to carry out the vision. God's provision is always ministry, men and money. God gives the vision, adds men, and money follows.

Doing things by compromise or by committee at times is not wrong, except that it is so easy for everyone to try to satisfy everyone and no one is pleased. God tells men to please Him, and He'll take care of everyone else.[7] The man who seeks to please God is most likely to have people pleased with him. *The closer a man is to God, the more a man of the people he becomes.*

Company executives and church leaders are most successful when in agreement with themselves and their goals, than when they try to agree with employees and congregations. It's far easier for a thousand to agree with one than one to agree with a thousand.

TOUCH AND METHOD

Every place Jesus went, He touched people and healed them. His method varied with the circumstances. The method always brought a reaction, but the touch brought the result. Perversion occurs through distortion when we teach the method and reward the reaction instead of teaching the touch and rewarding the result.

The method of the disciples was to evangelize in the marketplace. Today our message has not changed, but our method has. The contemporary marketplace is in media and communications, not just the open-air marketplace, so the Gospel is literally going around the world on television and radio. The touch and results are the same; the method and reactions are different.

CONSTANT AND INSTANT

Jesus' touch was constant; His method was instant. In our present society where instant gratification has become a way of life, some churches have "MacDonaldized" the Gospel, creating "microwave Christians" who are frustrated when God doesn't instantly fax them an answer to prayer. God is not concerned with the instant.

The Church is not a drive-through franchise dispensing cookie-cutter Christians. God is concerned about the constant.

His Word says the anointing "abides."[8] Jesus said, "If you abide in Me, and My words abide in you, you will ask what you desire, and it shall be done for you."[9] He did not say, "If you experience me and I experience you ... ."

The constant is the objective, and the instant is the subjective. When struggling in any situation, God can bring objectivity into life through prayer and the reading of His Word, because Christ is the "Counselor." When dealing with business, your family, a broken relationship, God's perspective will always be your most objective—and most correct.

By abiding in God, applying the constant, you will find yourself becoming "instant in season and out," ready at the right time with the right word, the right proposal, the right idea.

INTERNAL AND EXTERNAL

Man sees the outside, is concerned with talent and focuses on works. God looks on the heart,[10] is concerned with character and sees worth.

Abraham pitched his tents but built his altars.[11] Man creates a problem for himself when he begins to pitch his altars and build his tents. It is a difference in value. You can pitch personality, but you must build character.

In the church, God wants pillars who support the work, not posts who just pitch in. When the pressure comes, those who are "pillars" help stabilize the church. Those who are "posts" collapse under the weight of responsibility.

Principles are constant but personalities are instant. One who has "pitched" his personality can change in a minute. One who has built his character on principle is steadfast. *When the internal is godly, the external shows it.*

Facts follow faith. Faith determines what the facts will be.

In seeking God's Kingdom, the priorities are the constant, the touch, results, the internal and character.

What follows are the instant, the method, reactions, the external, talent and personality.

SUCCESS AND FAILURE

Success and failure are both common to man.

People have a natural fear of failure, based on the fear of death. We are preconditioned to failure because everything in the natural is subject to failure. Stars fall, earth quakes, seas rage, men lie, buildings fall and the earth grows old. Men spend millions of dollars trying to discover a way to escape failure.

There is one surefire way to overcome failure: Be successful.

God has a plan for success delineated in Joshua 1:7-8. You can meditate on it until it becomes real in your own heart.

God's plan is just two steps. First, be converted from the negative to the positive. From darkness to light, fear to faith, death to life. We must believe God is working for our highest good, that what He has promised, He will perform. This occurs when we are translated from the kingdom of Satan to the Kingdom of God.

Second, we must meditate on His Word and adhere to it. God's Word is the sole source of our faith and the absolute rule of our conduct. God's promise assures us that meditating on the Word to become a doer of it will bring success.[12]

The outcome, God says, is that "you may prosper wherever you go," you will deal wisely and have good success. Simple, but the challenge of a lifetime to enact. Acquiring wisdom and achieving success is not for the fainthearted or mediocre. Overcoming barriers in our lives is not always instantaneous, but, by seeking God's Kingdom first, change will begin.

The frustrations of the tensions between the two kingdoms, the struggle to balance the temporal and eternal, are resolved when we seek first the

There is one surefire way to overcome failure: Be successful.

eternal. Then all those things we seek in the temporal are added to us.

The second part of the verse, "and all these things shall be added to you,"[13] is where we get that piece of Heaven into our lives.

We erupt in praise to God when we realize Who Christ is and the limitlessness He gives us. We see God as God when we meet Him all alone, stripped of all physical accoutrements and assets. We rise from our knees and stand strong, bringing the eternal to bear on the temporal. We don't shrink from adversity, neither do we ignore reality.

Eternal hope transcends temporary circumstances.

God, through us, conquers all.

13

The Cost of Greatness

MATURITY DOESN'T COME WITH AGE, BUT BEGINS with the acceptance of responsibility. I usually follow that statement in meetings with: "That's why some men are more mature at seventeen than others are at forty-seven." Once, a woman on the front row burst out, "Forty-seven? You mean sixty-seven!"

True maturity and greatness in manhood begins with the acceptance of responsibility. You can see this in the epitome of the real man, Jesus. He didn't just accept responsibility to come in the flesh in accordance with the Father's will, but that in redemption He accepted responsibility for the sins of all mankind.

To fulfill the Father's will, Christ bore the sins of the whole world at Calvary. It's one thing to accept responsibility for your own actions, another to accept those of the most profligate and reprehensible sinners, to bear their guilt and shame, and endure their punishment when you are completely innocent and guiltless. Add to that the cumulative wickedness of all mankind, and you realize Jesus must be the Son of God to have borne such a burden. Most men can hardly bear their own guilt, much less take on that of the entire world.

Christ's greatness is intensified by His willingness to be the minister and servant of all mankind. He served men by becoming the Savior, offered redemption to all through His atonement at Calvary, and now serves humanity through meeting the needs of His Church as their Intercessor and answering all who call on His Name.

Christ taught that "whoever desires to become great among you, let him be your servant. And whoever desires to be first among you, let him be your slave."[1]

Greatness comes through serving. The more you serve, the greater you become.

Serving is not trying to compensate for what others didn't do. Serving involves meeting others' needs, through love, which is an expression of selflessness.

The Lord's greatness was seen when He took the towel to wash Peter's feet. Peter told Him he needed not only his feet, but his entire person washed. That is what Jesus came to do, but in spirit. What He was doing for Peter's feet was only a symbol of Jesus' ministry. His humility, exemplified in such a servile act, authenticated Christ's teaching. He taught not only in word but in example.[2]

Jesus accepted the responsibility of serving. His own words still certify His ministry: "The Son of Man did not come to be served, but to serve."[3] Due to His mercies, we daily exercise faith in Him, pray, and believe that He will answer. He has even charged the angels to be ministering spirits to those who will inherit salvation.[4] *His benevolence knows no bounds, His grace no barrier, His love no end.*

Billy Graham accepted the responsibility of serving as Christ's ambassador throughout the world. It meant growing into the responsibility personally, ministerially, culturally, spiritually, morally and in his trustworthiness. Billy's greatness is apparent in the multitude to whom he has ministered and the longevity of his ministry.

Serving produces greatness in the world's system, as well as God's Kingdom. General Motors Corporation became one of the world's greatest companies because it served so many people. A small company in the beginning, it grew and generated greatness as it provided cars, equipment, and accessories.

Maturity doesn't come with age, but begins with the acceptance of responsibility.

Fame and greatness are not synonymous. There is a vast difference between Madonna and Mother Teresa. Madonna is famous. Mother Teresa is great.

"Your care for others is the measure of your greatness," Jesus said.[5]

The maturation process begins with faith, adds moral excellence, knowledge, then self-control, patience, developing godliness, brotherly kindness, and to all those—love.[6] To begin the process, accepting responsibility for sin is necessary. The negative must be handled before the positive can follow.

THE TEST OF MANHOOD

Eve succumbed to the three basic temptations in the "original sin." Look at Adam's part in it. God's directive to Adam was not to eat the fruit of the tree of life in the middle of the Garden of Eden. Adam gave the commandment to Eve. The devil did not confront Adam, but deceived Eve into eating the fruit. Rationalizing his behavior to justify his action, Adam rejected God's will and word, and joined Eve in her insurrection.[7]

Later, when Adam and Eve heard God's voice in the garden calling them to fellowship, they hid. God confronted Adam who admitted he was hiding due to his guilt and fear. Consider what Adam did at this point. God asked Adam a direct question: "Did you take of the tree I told you not to?"

God was dealing with Adam as a Father to a son. God wanted Adam to be a man. "Answer the question: Did you or didn't you?"

"The woman *You* gave me, she gave me of the tree and I did eat," Adam answered, and failed the test of manhood. Adam blamed God for his trouble. Adam refused to accept responsibility for his actions. Adam's reply set the course for men from then until now.

Some Bible scholars advocate that the reason for Adam's expulsion from Eden wasn't due to Adam's sin, but to his refusal to accept responsibility for his actions. They base this on the idea that God would have forgiven Adam if he had confessed, repented, and asked for forgiveness in integrity of heart. He did not, making it impossible for God to leave him in the garden.

In Adam's sin against God, Adam's nature changed. The evidence was in his statement, "The woman whom You gave to be with me, she gave me of the tree, and I ate."[8] Adam's accusation against God to justify himself displayed his complicity with Satan, the "accuser of the brethren."[9] In Adam's accusation against God, he denied God's sovereignty. God's sovereignty exists in His absolute right to determine what is right and wrong for His creation, man.

God created Adam as a son. God dealt with Adam as with a son. When Adam sinned, the full revelation of the nature of God as a heavenly Father had to wait for the advent of another Adam, God's "only begotten Son." Jesus, as the "last Adam," brought the truth of God as Father, and through His Sonship enabled men to become sons of God by being born of God's Spirit.

God expects us in our manhood to accept responsibility.

A basic tenet of fathering is teaching children to accept responsibility for their actions. Discipline to enforce correction is one pattern to teach obedience. But fathers confront their sons before meting out discipline to make sure the son understands what is happening.

An Army colonel tells his eight-year-old son not to play ball between the houses on the base, for fear of breaking a window. But a window is found broken. Before disciplining his son, the colonel asks his son if he did it. Many times a father will know a child has done something, but it is vital that the father give the child the opportunity to admit it so his child can accept responsibility for his own actions.

Greatness comes through serving. The more you serve, the greater you become.

The discipline the son receives becomes based on his honest admission of guilt. To lie, equivocate, deny, or pass blame on another to absolve himself would call for harsher punishment than an honest admission of disobedience. The father would be more pleased with the son's integrity and acceptance of responsibility than shirking it.

ACCEPTING RESPONSIBILITY

Saul. Adam was the first man not to accept responsibility, but he certainly was not the last. Inseparably linked to the love of truth is the willingness to accept responsibility for what is true. When Saul was confronted with his sin of offering a sacrifice, usurping the priest's place, and not waiting for the prophet Samuel, Saul accused Samuel of being at fault because he did not arrive when Saul thought he should.[10] Saul's making the sacrifice offended God. His refusal to repent caused his rejection as king.

David. King David, on the other hand, grew in stature and in favor with God and man. David took full responsibility for what God commanded him concerning Israel, her enemies, God's people, and his own actions. When the prophet Nathan confronted him about his adultery with Bathsheba, David repented in sackcloth and ashes.[11] *Because David loved truth, he applied it to his life.*

In Zigklag, David's decisions led to the capture of the families of his band of followers. It was the low point of his life. His men, so loyal, steadfast in devotion, fighting to take him to the throne of Israel, now talked of stoning him. Prayerful rather than prideful, David confessed his wrong decisions, sought God's forgiveness and mercy, and encouraged himself in the Lord. God assured David that all the kidnapped families would be recovered. David's manhood, proven in crisis, brought the recovery of everything, including his stature in the sight of his men.[12]

Paul. The Apostle Paul took responsibility for the revelation of the Church, which God gave him while Paul was caught up in an exalted third heaven. Paul carried the fledgling young churches prayerfully in his heart and mind. He is the same who confessed he was the "chiefest of sinners" and accepted responsibility for his violent actions against Christians before his conversion.[13] Paul accepted the responsibility of being a role model for every male believer in his day, saying, "Follow my example, as I follow the example of Christ."[14] We still do.

Men Today. Athletes who have fame and fortune as a result of their ability and prowess must accept the responsibility it entails. Young men and women admire and emulate them. Refusing to accept responsibility as a role model for the young is disregarding societal duty.

Fathers who tell their children, "Don't do as I do, do as I say," are absolving themselves of responsibility to set a pattern of behavior to imitate. Children may not always listen to you, but they will always imitate you.

When a man finally accepts responsibility for his own actions it not only changes his destiny but also that of others.

Jack King has worked, prayed, traveled and served with me all over the world. He came to the ministry with a remarkable testimony.

"Execution Style Murder" screamed newspaper headlines when Jack's father was found murdered by gun shots to the face. For years, Jack carried a gun and spent most of his time planning to bring to justice the man who murdered his dad. A former U.S. Army Drill Sergeant, Jack had a rugged toughness that translated into a keen sense of hatred for the killer and a thirst for revenge. Worst of all, he believed he knew who the killer was—a business associate of his father's.

Then Jack was converted. Jesus Christ transformed his life, releasing him from his intense hatred. But that hurt of his dad's murder lingered in his heart. One evening during a church service, he heard God's Word that if he didn't forgive, God wouldn't forgive him. At that moment, he prayed and asked God to forgive him for the hatred and murderous attitude he once had. He believed God heard and answered his prayer, but was unprepared for the immediate test God gave.

A few evenings later, his wife asked him to go to the market. Driving through the darkness, he saw a commotion from a fire on the next street.

Children may not always listen to you, but they will always imitate you.

As Jack drew closer, he recognized the warehouse where he had found his murdered father, now owned by the man Jack believed responsible for the execution.

Thinking, "It serves him right," Jack continued driving. However a "small voice" told him to go find that man and ask his forgiveness. He left the store and started home but found he could not silence that inner voice. He turned down the other street.

Getting out of his car at the spot where his father had died, Jack walked up the darkened alley to examine the chaos and see if he could find the business associate. In the flashing lights of the fire trucks, Jack saw another man standing in the darkness with him. Peering through the dark and smoke, Jack saw it was the very man he was after. Summoning every fiber of strength, he took a step toward him and asked, "Do you know me?"

"You look familiar."

"I'm Jack King."

Despite the darkness, Jack could see the man blanch with fear. He thought Jack had set the fire and now wanted to complete his revenge.

"God has changed my life," Jack said, "and I've come to ask you to forgive me for accusing you of my dad's murder. I'm trying to make things right. I need to ask you to forgive me for my hatred and for haunting you these past years. And for trying to ruin your life, your family and your career."

"Yeah, well—"

"I want you to forgive me for all the harm I've done to you. Please forgive me."

"No problem. You're forgiven."

"No, I mean really forgive me, not just say it. I never want to offend you or hold ill-will against you again. I want you to know that."

There was a long pause. Finally, the man let out a deep sigh and affirmed his forgiveness for Jack. Jack held out his hand, and they shook on it.

> A basic tenet of fathering is teaching children to accept responsibility for their actions.

With the awkwardness now over, Jack spent the next half hour telling his former enemy of how Christ had changed his life and what it meant to his family. The conversation ended with Jack praying the prayer of salvation with the man. Then Jack impulsively threw an arm around the man, and the two wept on each other's shoulders as the years of hurt, hatred and fear melted away.

On the way home, Jack's tears were almost a hazard to his driving. The emotion-packed encounter had brought such release. Jack had the joy of knowing he had acted like a "real man." To this day, Jack King is a new man. After all his "tough guy" days in football, the Army and his career, Jack learned that accepting responsibility for his actions and making restitution gave him a sense of manhood not found anywhere else.

God never asked Jack to take on the responsibility of his father's murder. God is taking care of that. "'Vengeance is Mine, I will repay,' says the Lord."[15] Jack's responsibility was to have a pure heart, full of forgiveness toward others, so God would fully forgive him.

Individually or corporately, being responsible determines greatness of life.

Our fame, fortune, prestige and power don't tell the tale; the manner in which we serve does. And that is built on the responsibility we're willing to accept. "Whoever desires to be first among you, let him be your servant"[16] is the Word of Him Who serves as Savior and Lord.

14

The Winning Strategy

KNOWLEDGE IS THE ACQUIRING OF FACTS, understanding is the interpreting of facts, and wisdom is the application of facts. Of these three, God calls wisdom the "principle thing."[1] There is no area in life that does not benefit from wisdom.

God admonishes us to ask Him for wisdom, and promises to give it generously without finding fault, or looking for an excuse not to answer our request.[2] The Lord visited Solomon in a dream and asked what He could give him. Solomon asked for discernment in judging the people. Solomon's request so pleased God that He promised him riches and honor unequaled in all history, plus a wise and discerning heart.[3]

The Bible mentions two kinds of wisdom.

Human wisdom is "earthy, sensual, demonic."[4]

Divine wisdom comes "from above." The characteristics of this wisdom stem from the character of God, "first pure, then peaceable, gentle, willing to yield, full of mercy and good fruit, without partiality and without hypocrisy."[5] The results of godly wisdom are a long good life, riches, honor, pleasure and peace.[6] In other words, *godly wisdom provides for a man's total needs.*

The fear of the Lord is the prerequisite for acquiring godly wisdom. The fear of the Lord is a reverent awe of God and causes a hatred of evil. To fear God means to acknowledge God for who He is, in all His power and majesty. "The fear of the Lord is the beginning of wisdom."[7] When we fear the Lord, we flee iniquity, which is wise living.

Solomon illustrated his fear of God before asking for wisdom. He recognized that God was the Creator, Who gave him his life and kingdom, and the God of the people he ruled.

You have shown great mercy to your servant David my father, because he walked before you in truth, in righteousness, and in uprightness of heart with You; You have continued this great kindness for him, and You have given him a son to sit on his throne, as it is this day. Now, O Lord my God, You have made Your servant king.[8]

Because of Solomon's fear of the Lord, God granted his request for wisdom and then some.

Adam was given a spirit of wisdom, but he lost the fear of the Lord and sinned, and his wisdom was blighted. Jesus, the Last Adam, once again had the "Spirit of wisdom and understanding."[9] Through Him, that wisdom is available to us. Jesus "become for us wisdom."[10] Through Christ, God freely gives us wisdom.[11] Christ enables us to know the manifest wisdom of God.[12]

People who reject Christ are left with only human wisdom. By rejecting the fear of the Lord, they reject true wisdom.[13] The Bible calls them fools.[14]

APPLYING WISDOM IN LIFE

It is basic wisdom to prepare for the future and foolishness not to. Jesus illustrated this with a story about a man who was to be discharged from a management position. Concerned about his future, he discounted each creditor's account before he left the firm. His strategy was to find favor with one of them so they would employ him when he was fired.[15] Jesus commended the man, not for his chicanery, but for the basic wisdom he used to secure his future.

We often flunk the basics. Failing to prepare for your future through dropping out of school is one thing; to flunk the preparation for discharge from this life by rejecting the

Bible is another. If a man knows that one day he is going to be discharged from this life, failure to prepare for what comes next is foolishness.

First in intention is last in execution is the principle. On a recent trip, I planned to go to Brisbane, Perth and Sydney. That was my first intention. However, I had to arrange for a visa, buy tickets, pack bags, arrange travel, coordinate personnel, fly there, and finally arrive—my first intention was the last thing I executed.

Most people plan for big events "first things first." It is wisdom to begin planning what occurs after the event, then work back to the present. Too often people plan for meetings, weddings, special events, and start at the beginning, only to come to the end and ask for volunteers to help clean up or pack—perhaps doing it themselves because of faulty planning.

The first intention in any life is to go to Heaven, but it is the last thing done. Everything between then and now is preparation. From now until you arrive, you continue with life's plan to make it happen.

The famous basketball coach John Wooden put it, *"Failure to prepare is preparation for failure."*

True in sport. True in life and death. This is basic wisdom.

Consider what happens to those without wisdom. Satan has no wisdom. He has knowledge but lacks true wisdom because he has no fear of the Lord. Satan lost his fear of the Lord, was cast out of Heaven and lost his wisdom.[16] The man who has godly wisdom has dominion over the devil. The man who has only earthly wisdom invites the devil and the world to exercise dominion over him.

All sin is a form of insanity. Satan is the most insane being of all because he still believes he can defeat God. Those who succumb to his temptations adopt behaviors that are utterly unreasonable and, therefore, technically insane.

> **Knowledge is the acquiring of facts, understanding is the interpreting of facts, and wisdom is the application of facts.**

Doug Stringer is a minister who started on the streets of Houston and now has a network of outreaches all over the world. He sent me a video recently with interviews of young men who practice homosexuality in the inner city of Houston. Teenaged men said on-camera that they continued in their promiscuity even though they knew some of their partners might have AIDS. An AIDS sufferer said on-camera, "I only wish I could tell them what it is like—the trauma, terror, suffering—and warn them to stop before it is too late."

We fall prey to the insanity of sin, at times even shocking ourselves.

I counseled a man who had committed adultery but was reconciling with his wife. Nancy and I took them to lunch one day and talked about his affair. His wife turned and asked him, "Didn't you think of me or the children when you were doing it?"

He shook his head and said, "The only thing I thought of was my own pleasure." *Sin never thinks of the consequences, only the pleasure of the moment.*

This man never intended to hurt his wife or estrange his children. To do so was beyond reason. He loved them, but did it anyway.

God's strategy to deliver men from their folly is Calvary. There Jesus made the sacrifice so every man could be changed eternally and take dominion over sin, Satan and even death. Once we accept that sacrifice, we are candidates for receiving God's wisdom.

WISDOM – STRATEGY – VICTORY

God's wisdom is the key to gaining victory in almost every area of life. Think of wisdom as it relates to your marriage, business decisions, financial problems or health. Wisdom is the key to the problems confronting you.

One day as I was reading the prayer requests people send me, I noticed how often they used the word *victory*. They needed to overcome behaviors, difficulties, and afflictions, but referred to it as wanting *victory*.

It occurred to me that *victory* was a miscellaneous description for the solution to any need. "Victory in marriage" meant to reconcile with a separated mate. "Victory over finances" meant to get out of debt. "Victory in health" meant to be cured of something. They all wanted *victory*.

To obtain victory, a strategy is required. To acquire strategy, wisdom is necessary. Instead of asking for *victory,* these people needed to seek the prerequisite—wisdom. God's wisdom will give the strategy to obtain the victory.

Scripture tells of Syrian General Naaman who desperately sought a cure for his leprosy. when it was proffered, he almost refused the strategy necessary to be healed. A servant maid, carried captive to Syria from Israel, had suggested to her mistress, the wife of Naaman, that Naaman go to the prophet in Israel to be healed. Naaman went carrying jewels, money, and clothes to give as a payment for his recovery. When Naaman arrived at the prophet's home, the prophet didn't bother to meet Naaman, but sent his servant to tell him to dip in the Jordan River seven times. Naaman was incensed that the prophet would not meet him in person, but was simply told by a servant to dip in a muddy river. His pride suffered an indignity.

"I thought at least he would come out and talk to me! I expected him to wave his hand over the leprosy and call upon the name of the Lord his God, and heal me!" Naaman said.[17]

As he started to leave, filled with umbrage at the insult, one of his menial servants said, "If the prophet had told you to do some great thing, wouldn't you have done it? So you should certainly obey him when he says simply to go and wash and be cured."[18]

Those words halted Naaman. He considered the word of the servant, obeyed the command of the prophet, and was miraculously healed after his obedience.

The barriers Naaman had to overcome, we still stumble over: Predisposition, predetermination, and preconception. We imagine when and how our victory will occur. When the strategy is not what we envisioned, we have a difficult time accepting it. We can miss God's wisdom.

Naaman was guilty of "magical thinking." *God is a miracle worker, not a magician.*

A man involved in "magical thinking" requested me to pray for his marriage. For twenty-five years he had taken his wife for granted, had become careless in manner and dress, and failed to provide for his family. Meantime, his wife took care of the family, finished her education, established a career, and finally in hopelessness, filed for divorce. Suddenly desperate, he wanted someone to pray and heal him of twenty-five years of poor stewardship in his marriage. He wanted to erase by some magical process a quarter century of slack he had put into the marriage. God will resurrect marriages, but He does it through applied obedience, not by magic.

Remember, no man possesses his wife in marriage, he is only a steward of her love. He must prove himself a good steward of that love to maintain it over the years. I did pray for this man, but I also gave him a little wisdom.

"A man may ruin his chances by his own foolishness and then blame it on the Lord."[19]

In the world of sports, the God-given pattern of wisdom for victory is always used. Applied knowledge translates into wisdom, which develops strategies, which ensure victories. Sounds complex, but every great athlete knows it. *Take what you know, apply it with wisdom to develop a strategy, and you win!*

I heard a story years ago and remember it like this: Amos Alonzo Stagg was an all-time great football coach. While coaching from a wheelchair, a reporter told him, "You know more about football than any man alive. That must be why your team wins so much."

"You're wrong," said the venerable sportsman. "It's not what I know that wins games, it's what those young men on the field know." Stagg understood that execution wins games, and execution comes from practice, and practice is doing what you were taught until you excel at it.

IT'S THE GLORY WE DESIRE

Men are naturally drawn to victory. We are attracted by winners, which is why we like reading the sports pages of the newspaper. The sports page has winners, the front page has losers. The thrill of victory is in the glory that it brings. When a football team leaves a field victoriously, the locker room becomes charged with the winning atmosphere. Men revel in the glory of the "win." They revel in "success" because there is glory in victory.

It's the glory we desire, not just the victory.

Wisdom-strategy-victory-glory is God's pattern.

Failures can have purpose, and even a reward of sorts, but winning is always glorious. Winning teams, political parties, and game show contestants erupt in delirious celebration when victory occurs. Even conservative golfers, scientists and businessmen shed tears of joy on the day of their greatest feats.

Victory is always glorious. God gives grace to sinners, but glory to saints. *The glory is in the victory, the wisdom is in the strategy.*

Christian men and women pray for "victories" because they want the glory of the win. The Bible teaches us to "glory in the Lord."[20] God wants believers to go "from glory to glory."[21] No wonder He wants to give us wisdom. Since the glory is in the victory, to go from "glory to glory" we must go from "victory to victory."

Victory is revealed in public, but is developed in private.

Only victors know the hard, long, lonely, bruising hours all alone with only their desire. When a man wins the decathlon, or a young girl excels in gymnastics, none know better than they the rigors required. Too often the difference between winning and losing is in hundredths of a second or fractions of an inch. A wise man disciplines

> To obtain victory, a strategy is required. To acquire strategy, wisdom is necessary.

himself in developing a strategy to accomplish such a small thing. *Strategies are developed in private, victories are won in public.*

The levels of knowledge are assumption at the bottom, then knowledge, skill, and practice. The issue is not having the knowledge and skill to do something once, but putting it into practice. A lucky golfer may break par once, but a successful golfer does it consistently because it is a practice. Parenting, business, sports, investments, friendships, purchases, marriages—we need wisdom to practice victory in these and achieve every dream. *God-given dreams, in God-favored men, make a God-blessed world.*[22]

The value of wisdom is "better than rubies." Its worth exceeds that of gold or silver.[23] God does not give wisdom to the casual, slothful, indifferent or superficial inquirer. He reveals wisdom only to those who realize its value, seek it wholeheartedly, earnestly desire it, and value it as the priceless "gift" it is.

God promises to give wisdom, but says we must seek it first.

> *If you seek her as silver,*
> *And you search for her as for hidden treasures;*
> *Then you will understand the fear of the Lord,*
> *And find the knowledge of God.*
> *For the Lord gives wisdom;*
> *From His mouth come knowledge and understanding.*[24]

Wisdom lies below the surface of knowledge. You have to dig for it, but the reward is worth the effort!

15

Employed for Life

"ALL TRUTH IS PARALLEL."[1] WHAT IS FOUND IN the eternal has a parallel in the temporal. Rob Carman, a pastor friend, discovered this principle holds true in regard to employment. *Employment, both in the secular and sacred fields, creates production and momentum, but unemployment creates a stifling atmosphere.*

Rob's church had reached a plateau numerically after starting with a handful of people and growing to a congregation of approximately 1,500. The zeal, fervor and aggressiveness that had characterized the initial growth seemed to have lost momentum. The time he formerly had for prayer and study seemed to fill with increased counseling, moral contests among members and family problems.

Perplexed and distressed, he was meditating on the Scriptures when he remembered an article he had seen in the newspaper days before. A report cited statistics of what happens to a community when unemployment rises. He realized that what happened in the community was similar to what was happening in the community of the church. The effects of high unemployment primarily and fundamentally cause the loss of self-esteem in men. *When a man cannot provide for himself or his own, he is robbed of his dignity.*

The loss of employment affects the individual, his family and society in general. The resulting societal evils, including drugs, promiscuity, disease and welfare abuse, are a plague on the citizenry, who are then required to meet the needs for counsel, medication and social assistance. At the root of the problem lies the fact that men were created in the image of God with abilities and creativity, and are required to produce. When a man's abilities are stifled and not used for gainful productivity, he will find a way to express them. *If a man's abilities and creativity cannot be expressed legally, he will find fulfillment illegally, immorally and illicitly.*

Rob explains, "When a man is robbed of his right to work, to earn an honest dollar for an honest day's work, he is made dependent on a system that violates him." In Third World nations and neighborhood ghettos with exaggerated unemployment, when worth and self-esteem are taken from men, they move into illegal or immoral activities to satisfy and fulfill themselves.

THE DANGER

Today, government agencies admit that drug dealing will never be stopped by merely legal methods. When a teenager pushing drugs walks down the street with money stuffed in his pockets, his value as a man is gratified to a great extent. He is gratified in his ability to earn money, in exercising his creativity to obtain it and in the productivity of making it. His method is morally and legally wrong, but nevertheless, he feels fulfilled in his manhood.

The Bible lays down a work ethic for all society which says if you don't work, you don't eat.[2] The simple reason for the work ethic is the dignity of man. When God gave manna in the wilderness, He could have given it a month at a time. Instead, He gave it on a daily basis so work was provided and dignity was given. Without working for what he is eating, a man is living off someone else's dignity.

Spirituallyunemployed Christians have "religion" that offers them none of the excitement of the spiritually employed.

In reference to Satan, Jesus taught that the thief comes to steal, kill and destroy.[3] Stealing ability, killing creativity and destroying productivity is devilish.

America today is in danger of destruction, not from its enemies, but due to shifting from a productive society to a consumer-oriented society. The nation has shifted from a position of wealth and strength to become the world's largest debtor nation. "Japan bashing" is in vogue because of Japan's financial power in America and the world, but the truth is that Japan has simply out-produced the U.S. The Japanese work ethic is as strong as or stronger than ever, while the work ethic in America is almost in eclipse.

In other countries, socialism teaches men to depend on the system to provide for them. Even worse, totalitarian dictators assume divine status in their own eyes and promulgate that to their citizens. Socialism in all its forms is a proven failure. In New Zealand, their "dole" system has almost crippled the country. Communism, another failure, was a feudal system. Party bosses were lords and citizens simply serfs.

The welfare system in America is a type of socialism. What started idealistically as a way to free people from "poor farms" has enslaved those it meant to save. The "poor farm," where families were sent to live until work was available, became a symbol for failure. Those using it were considered second- or third-class citizens. Welfare was established to replace the farms, as a temporary help until recipients could become productive again. Today, rather than using welfare to prepare for work, many recipients make more on welfare than they would working for minimum wage. They are robbed of a reason to go to work and be productive. The result is mentally and morally emasculated manhood.

High unemployment creates compound difficulties that require more than the citizenry can pay for. Unemployment of 25 percent in communities is considered excessive, propagates the problems and distresses and perpetuates a "poverty complex."

Experts say the welfare system teaches people to violate the program to provide for themselves. In some cities, it saps the very vitality of the city's economy. Exacerbating the city's financial plight, the results are thoroughfares with potholes, garbage and trash littering streets and vacant lots, graffiti disgracing vehicles and buildings and indifference to the blight by elected officials.

THE PROBLEM IN THE CHURCH

A parallel to the secular is found in the sacred. Consider the estimates that rate between 75-80 percent of church members as only "hearers" but not "doers." "Hearers" of the Word want the church to support them rather than them support the church. They make the church employ a form of "spiritual socialism." With a "welfare mentality," they depend on the pastor as the source of all wisdom and rely on church programs to maintain them. The pastor, not the Bible, becomes their source of faith and rule for conduct.

Without the fulfillment and satisfaction gained from service to the Lord, church members are robbed of their true value to the Kingdom of God and, as in the secular, turn to things illicit, immoral or illegal to provide for the void in their lives.

In the competition between the church and world, the world wins if the church cannot provide the quickening power of the Holy Spirit to make alive the reality of the Gospel, the joy of worship, the dynamism of preaching, the wonder of answered prayer, the "anointed high" from sharing truth or the splendor of fellowship with Jesus.

The Christlike don't discover their ministry gifts by sitting around analyzing someone else's teaching. Gifts become manifest in the process of ministering to others.

Sterile sermons cannot compete with crap tables in casinos. Pathetic prayers don't have the exhilaration of pornography. Boring church rituals are no match for football or baseball. Faked smiles at church socials don't have the dynamism of a rock concert.

Spiritually unemployed Christians have "religion" that offers them none of the excitement of the spiritually employed.

By definition, the spiritually employed are those men, and women, who have found the reality of a vital living relationship with Jesus Christ, have become a partaker of His Spirit, have been made alive through His indwelling life and have submitted themselves to His Word and will. Enlisted in an army to fulfill His commission to "make disciples," they are actively engaged in serving, exercising "serving gifts" and finding fulfillment and satisfaction of the highest order.

When such people attend church services, they are eager to learn, hungry to digest truth, delighted in worship and quick to discover new joys in helping others. They desire others to share the same relationship with the Lord Jesus Christ they have discovered and experienced. And, they are in the minority. It's the 80-20 principle.

Most people attend church meetings to "be blessed," not to "be a blessing." Selfishly desiring only what benefits them, they become dissatisfied when their expectations are not met. Perhaps the pastor's message isn't up to standard, the music isn't suiting, ushers aren't polite. When things aren't pleasing to them, they leave disgruntled and unhappy. However, when people arrive with the attitude of serving God, worshiping Christ, ministering to the Lord and His Church, they leave blessed, no matter what happens.

Businessmen realize that 20 percent of their clients provide 80 percent of their work. School teachers know that 20 percent of the students create 80 percent of the problems. And pastors know that approximately 20 percent of the people do 80 percent of the work of the church. The rest are spiritually unemployed.

In the void of productivity, the unemployed become more of a problem than a solution. The excitement, zeal and

> To a real man, spiritual employment brings dignity, prosperity, authority, charity and tranquility.

fervor of serving God diminish, and they look for the zest for life outside the church and the Lord's service.

At a recent men's event in Southern California, some teen-men stood to tell what they found exciting about life. With their hair pulled back and bound with a net, pegged pants, necklace chains, inscribed T-shirts and holding the biggest Bibles they could find, each, in turn, told the hundreds of men gathered that they had formerly been gang members, running with guns and knives, but since becoming Christian, they have found the most exciting life of all. In short speeches punctuated with Scriptures recited from memory, these young men charged the crowd with their enthusiasm, telling of their daring to go back to the gangs and share the life of Christ.

"There is no high like the spiritual high that Jesus gives," one said. "The guys I used to know stopped running with me. When I had a gun and knife, nobody was afraid of me, but since I found Jesus, they're all afraid of me. Nobody wants to get in my car with me because they're afraid I'll try to convert them. And I will!"

These young men are filled with excitement for the Lord, busy about the Lord's business, and no longer have time for things illicit, immoral or illegal. They are spiritually employed in the greatest work on earth.

And they're right—there is no "high" like that which comes from praying with or for someone who is helped eternally. *Nothing can substitute for the thrill of seeing someone experience a newfound relationship with Jesus Christ.*

DO THE WORK OF AN EVANGELIST

The Apostle Paul gave Timothy a simple instruction that applies to all believers: "But you are watchful in all things, endure afflictions, do the work of an evangelist, fulfill your ministry."[4]

If this were a job description for Billy Graham, it might have said, "Be an evangelist." But Paul worded it differently: "Do the work of an evangelist." He commands all of us to tell people about Jesus in order to "fulfill" our ministry. Why? People in the secular realm may go to seminars or read books to find where they fit in the job market, but God's Kingdom doesn't work that way.

The Christlike don't discover their ministry gifts by sitting around analyzing someone else's teaching. Gifts become manifest in the process of ministering to others. By doing the work of an evangelist, the Spirit of God manifests our ministry and motivational gifts and brings us the realization of our temperament.

Inactivity produces nothing. When we actively pursue truth in word and deed, productivity results.

Reading the Bible is being spiritually employed. Praying with your wife is being spiritually employed. So is sharing your faith with another, visiting the sick and lonely and most of all, doing something to help another know Christ. Doing the work of an evangelist is vital.

Evangelistic work develops a pattern for life that necessitates a vital prayer life, bold identification with Christ and commonality with others in order to share with them. Men must see the necessity of the Kingdom harvest to retain—

- the value of their own personal salvation
- the true meaning of Calvary
- a hunger for God's Word
- a desire for God's reward
- the purpose of the Holy Spirit in life
- the reason for being a Christian
- to keep sight of eternity
- to maintain faithful stewardship of life

These attributes naturally spring from evangelism.

Rob Carman taught this principle to his congregation, and 92 percent of the members became spiritually employed in some kind of evangelistic work. They began testifying, witnessing to acquaintances and friends or to strangers on street corners, depending on their ministry gifts and began encouraging other Christians in home groups. In one year, those church members ministered individually to 150,000 people. That's employment!

The pastor was no longer the resolution of every problem, because the people were studying the Bible. He was free to return to his Bible study, praying and preaching. The pastor and people reaped earthly benefits of their employment—a sense of self-worth and dignity came by carrying out God's plan to be creative and productive.

When people become spiritually employed, the Kingdom of God on earth is released. To a real man, spiritual employment brings dignity, prosperity, authority, charity and tranquility.

"Therefore, my beloved brethren, be steadfast, immovable, always abounding in the work of the Lord, knowing that your labor is not in vain in the Lord."[5]

16

Financial Freedom

CARMAN CALLED ME LATE ONE EVENING WHEN we were both in hotels, thousands of miles apart. He was troubled by an earlier conversation he had with a friend.

Carman is more than a Gospel singer in my estimation. He is a musical genius. He raised the art of story-telling in music to a new form with drama, staging, sound, melody and lyric. His is a blend of truth in song that attracts people by the multiplied thousands to his concerts. For this gifted man to be troubled by anything drew my immediate attention.

A friend had chided Carman for using his gift for the "Gospel circuit" instead of taking it into the arena of pop music. His friend contended that Carman could become famous and rich, win Grammys, and later in life, do something for the Lord "after making a name for himself." The friend thought this was better than spending the best years of life traveling and ministering the Gospel where there wasn't much money or fame.

"Why waste your talent?" the friend had asked.

"Ed, I don't want to waste my talent," Carman told me. Then he answered his own question as he said, *"To me, a waste is taking the best of what you have and using it on the devil's work, then giving what you have left to the Lord."*

"You're absolutely right!" I said.

Investing your energy, ingenuity, initiative, ability and creativity in the Kingdom of God is wisdom, not waste. Giving to God is never a waste. When we give money to God in an offering, we give for many reasons, but we always give to Him, not the man taking the offering. *By our giving, we gain something that is impossible to gain any other way.*

The use of money is the acid test of character in a real man. The worldly philosophy of Carman's friend is something people have believed for years, that to give God their best robs them of what is best for them. Nothing could be further from the truth. Giving to God brings His favor, worth more than anything anyone could buy or gain.

Israel battled this attitude. At first, when God brought the Israelites out of Egypt's bondage, their gratitude knew no bounds. Moses told them they were to build a tabernacle in the wilderness, and they were so generous, he had to restrain them from giving more. They laid their lives and all they possessed on the Lord's altar in worship.[1]

But centuries later, the prophet Malachi thundered an indictment from God to the offspring of those previous generations. Once generous to a fault, they were now bringing the sick, weak and maimed of their flocks and herds to offer on the altar. A young generation, they never knew Egypt or the miracles God performed to set their fathers free from slavery. They still had the external accoutrements of their worship but had lost the internal power of God's presence. As their hearts hardened toward Him, they saw nothing wrong with keeping the best for themselves, reinvesting it in their worldly businesses, and giving the leftovers to God.

"Offer that to your governor and see what he will do about it," God said through Malachi. "If then I am the Father. Where is my honor?"[2]

Their miserly offerings were a dishonor to Jehovah God, their Savior and Deliverer. The real waste was their whole lives. Giving God the dregs of life is shameful, selfish and sinful. Giving yourself to God is your greatest honor.

GIVE GOD YOUR BEST

In Jesus' parable, a Pharisee prayed self-righteously in public, and a publican prayed humbly in private. Jesus said the publican was justified and the Pharisee was not. The Pharisee, in his self-righteousness, had little to give but much to boast about, while the publican had nothing to boast about and only himself to give.[3]

In the house of Simon the leper, a woman with an alabaster box showered its priceless contents upon Jesus, anointing His feet and wiping them with her hair. She lavished herself and her most precious possession on her Lord.

Some of Jesus' disciples complained, saying, "To what purpose is this waste? For this fragrant oil might have been sold for much and given to the poor."[4] (John records this statement as coming from Judas who held the purse with the money.[5] Like many treasurers, Judas became ego-identified with the money, developed a possessive attitude toward it, and his covetousness later motivated him to betray Jesus for profit, a profit he never realized because the bitterness of betrayal turned him to suicide. The irony is that Judas protested the "waste" of priceless possessions on Christ but wasted his own most precious possession—his life.)

The Lord answered His disciples by reminding them: "For you have the poor with you always, but Me you do not have always."[6]

Robert Schuller built the Crystal Cathedral amid carping critics who said the money was better spent caring for the poor. Yet if the money had been used to help the poor, we would still have as many poor to care for today, but not the beautiful monument to the glory of God. How many men throughout the world have been attracted to the Gospel through the Cathedral, and how many have been strengthened through that ministry over the years?

Giving your best to God is not a waste—it is a glory! Jesus taught that when you have the opportunity to do something that will glorify God, do it. God is worthy of our very best, and He requires it.

Many drama critics have never produced a play. Many caustic sports writers have never played the game. Most pundits who second-guess politicians

God is worthy of our very best, and He requires it.

have never run for office. In the same way, most of those who criticize the Gospel have never attempted to do God's service. Generally, it is the "have-nots" finding fault with the "haves."

Don't let someone's faultfinding become your stumbling block. *Don't let some critic keep you from giving your best to God.*

Nothing lavished on Jesus is ever wasted. Whatever is given will always have a return. God is debtor to no man; therefore, no man can put God in his debt.[7] The Lord always gives more in return. This frees men to give liberally,[8] knowing they cannot outgive God.

Jesus didn't discourage riches nor condemn those who were rich. He taught the deceit of riches, which is:

1) the tendency to trust in riches instead of in God
2) being deceived into thinking riches bring happiness and health
3) being seduced by thinking no matter how much you have, it is never enough.

The real man doesn't rely on riches but on God. He doesn't expect happiness from riches but from friendships. He doesn't crave more but finds that "godliness with contentment is great gain."[9] Jesus gave all, His very life. Through His example, we know liberality is a mark of largeness in manhood.

A man reveals the condition of his heart by his attitude toward money. Jesus sat in temples, watching people give their offerings. "Where your treasure is, there your heart will be also," He said.[10]

THE RIGHT ATTITUDE

Our attitude in giving is sure to be tested. I once received an official-looking invitation to join a class-action suit to recover monies from Jim Bakker and the defunct PTL Ministries. Nancy and I had given monies to the ministry.

Now we were asked to sue Jim Bakker to recover what we had given. Nancy and I agreed to throw the letter away. When we invested in that ministry, we gave to God, not Jim. If I were to sue, I would have to sue God!

Contributing money to ministries is a joy. In giving, the offering is always to God, and any blessing or return benefit will come from God, not man.

I learned my lesson years ago. A pastor named Gerald and I were crossing the Puget Sound on a ferry, going from his hometown of Port Orchard to Seattle, to attend a gathering of men and ministers. In the final week of a forty-day fast, being very sensitive to God's Spirit, I felt a strong urge to give Gerald one hundred dollars from my billfold. It was the only money I had. With the giving came a surge of well-being, expansiveness, completeness, both from the obedience and the generous nature of it. I felt a great sense of accomplishment.

Going home from the meeting, Gerald said, "Ed, it's good you gave me that hundred because I gave it to the minister in the meeting who fell off his ladder, broke his arm and didn't have money for doctor bills. I figured he needed it more than I did."

As he spoke, I became upset with him. No, I was mad. That was my last hundred, and when I gave it to him, I never expected he would give it away. My expansiveness, well-being and completeness shrank to nothing because he gave my money away. How dare he?

About that time, I heard the still small voice of the Holy Spirit in my mind and heart bringing me the words of Jesus.

"Did I tell you to give it?" He asked.

"Yes, Lord."

"Did you give it to Me?"

"Yes, Lord."

"Your reward is in your obedience to Me and does not rest on what others do with what I tell you to give."

Okay, that was it. Once given—out of my control.

> Non-tithers are similar to nonvoters— they are both irresponsible.

From that moment to this, I have never worried about what others do with what I give. At times, with the smallest urging, I even give to those I am not sure will deal right-eously with my gift. They will give an account to God, not to me, for their disposition of the monies.

Just because some bankers are guilty of fraud doesn't stop me from banking my money. Just because some of my tax money may find its way into someone's pocket, I don't quit paying taxes. And though there may be ministers who have used the gifts of God's people lustfully, selfishly and personally, that doesn't stop me from giving to God. My responsibility to God is not built on someone else's relation-ship to Him. I don't deliberately set out to give irresponsibly, capriciously or carelessly, but I give responsibly and liberally, as pleasing to God.

THE TITHE AND THE OFFERING

Tithes are the monies we give God before the offerings, the "firstfruit" of earnings or wealth, which always belongs to Him.[11] "Honour the Lord with thy substance,"[12] is a com-mand, not an invitation. People who do not tithe live off the blessings of the church but repudiate its claims through their actions. Non-tithers are similar to nonvoters—they are both irresponsible.

The Church is not a beggar, pleading with people to part with their money, nor are ministers mendicants begging alms.

The prophet Malachi thundered his indictment against Israel for robbing God, "Will a man rob God?"[13] But how can you rob someone of what is not theirs? Understand this:

- The tithe is the Lord's.[14]
- The tithe is the Lord's and not ours, so if we do not give the tithe, we rob God.
- The tithe is the Lord's, so when we give it, we really have not given anything of our own until we give above the tithe.

- When we give to the Lord beyond our tithes, we enter into true sowing and reaping.

God promises to save tithers from disasters the devourer plans.[15] But when you give offerings, something will be "given to you; good measure, pressed down, and shaken together, and running over,"[16] whether tangible or intangible. *Tangible gifts can have incredibly rich intangible returns.*

Ruben is a great example. Ruben and his wife attended a "Sweetheart Meeting" where, at the end of the meeting, I asked couples who desired help in their marriages to come forward for prayer. I didn't know him and his wife, but something about them caught my attention.

"When was the last time you took your wife on a honeymoon?" I asked Ruben.

"I have never taken my wife on a honeymoon," he said.

"At this point," Ruben wrote later, "you graciously blessed us with the money in your pocket, so we could go on our first honeymoon." I had reached in my pocket and handed them all my travel allowance—$220.

Ruben wrote weeks later to say they had never gone on a honeymoon because they were never married! Living together for seven years, and having been Christians for just nine months, they had stopped having sex two months earlier until they could save enough to be married.

"With eight children between us," he wrote, "saving money was hard, especially since I was unemployed and a recovering drug addict. When I was saved and delivered from drugs, I chose to depend on my Lord for everything we did. We had been praying earnestly for the money to get married when we went to the meeting."

They married three days later, on Valentine's Day. The money covered the license and three nights at a hotel. But here's the amazing part:

Men cannot compensate by the sacrifice of prayer for what they lose through the disobedience of not being faithful in tithes and offerings.

"We came to your meeting with enough money to cover our gas and parking," he wrote "Well, as you were taking the offering, I remembered I had $2.20. The Holy Spirit spoke to me and said, 'Who is your Provider, who do you trust?' Needless to say, I put my $2.20 in the offering ... and then we were blessed with the miracle. What an awesome move of God!"

The principle Ruben's obedience illustrates is profound. *You gain by giving what you cannot buy with money.*

The intangible results Ruben received far outweighed any value of the tangible gift.

Ruben gave his last $2.20 and received a hundred times more in return, plus a new marriage, edified children, respect as a man, increased faith in God and a measure of manhood he never had before.

Givers gain when God causes contracts to come their way, employers to decide in their favor, children to find a godly hero—an unlimited range of intangible blessings God generously gives, in addition to tangible financial returns. Out of a heart of gratitude, blessed men then continue to give generously to God's work on earth.

The process started with God giving His best, Jesus Christ. It continues when a man surrenders his life in commitment to the Lord, visibly expressed in tithes and offerings.

What a great statement of love and trust toward God, to give the very means by which we live—money. *Money, like sex, is an expression of love, made for loving and giving, not lusting and getting.*

GIVE YOURSELF FIRST

Giving money follows the giving of self.[17] When Zaccheus became a believer in Jesus, his desire to make restitution for what he had fraudulently garnered was the evidence of his changed heart. The condition of his heart was shown in the use of his money.[18] Restitution was not a word but an action.

In a later story, Cornelius, the centurion, qualified to become the gateway of the Gospel to the Gentiles, by his praying ... and by his offerings.[19] Later still, the letter to the church at Corinth tells how those who willingly gave of their means to support the Gospel had first given themselves to God.[20]

Jesus said, "Make friends for yourselves by unrighteous mammon, that when you fail, they may receive you."[21] He did not mean to buy friendships but to use money to make friends for eternity. *By tithes, gifts and contributions, the Gospel is preached, men become sons of God and friends are made for eternity.*

Money is a means of doing great good. Good and great fruit follow obedience in giving. God never cursed a fig tree because it bore so much fruit that some of it fell to the ground and spoiled. He cursed it only when it bore no fruit.[22]

Obedience is the evidence of love, and manifestation is based on obedience. "To obey is better than sacrifice."[23] Jesus said, "He who has My commandments and keeps them, it is he who loves Me. And he who loves Me will be loved by My Father, and I will love him and manifest Myself to him."[24]

At a Milwaukee conference during the 1984 recession, I intended to pray for men in financial distress. During the time of ministry, I asked how many of those having difficulties had not been faithful in tithes and offerings. Almost 100 percent admitted they had not been consistent.

At that moment, I realized something. These men were trying to compensate by the sacrifice of prayer for what they lost through the disobedience of not being faithful in tithes and offerings.

It can't be done. They needed to faithfully contribute to the Gospel and trust God for divine compensation.

God's abundance is without limit. *God puts no limitation on faith, and faith puts no limitation on God.*[25]

Jesus memorialized the woman who expended her most priceless possession on Him, stating, "Wherever this gospel is preached in the whole world, what this woman has done will also be told."[26] What He did for her, He will do for you.

17

Positive Stress

AFTER RESTLESSLY PREPARING THROUGH THE night for a men's event, I called my office one morning only to find some confusion and disorganization. No sooner was that resolved than a crisis call came from a member of a board on which I serve. I was already under pressure that day to complete a chapter of this book and had a minister from overseas coming to see me. I was undecided on how to divide my time. Then a friend called for counsel. Each of my children called in succession. Paul had a business problem. Lois, a deputy district attorney, was concerned about an upcoming trial. Joann was having difficulties with her sons. The pressure was on.

At midmorning, I still had not gone to the beach for my normal prayer time. When I finally made my way downstairs, I found Nancy sifting through a stack of prayer requests that I was sure represented every ill ever visited on mankind. The newspaper on the counter caught my eye as I opened the cupboard to pour myself a bowl of cereal, which I discovered we didn't have. It was the day after statewide elections, and from the looks of the headlines, we would have some grim years ahead of us in government. I growled something about the world falling apart and felt the air around me tingle with static electricity.

Calmly and sweetly, Nancy looked up from the table and said with a smile, *"A wise man once said, 'Pressure always magnifies.'"*

She was right! I knew my next sequence of thought. The world was terrible—I was doing it no good—there was no reason for me to be alive—everyone around me was in distress—and I was worthless as a friend, father, minister and counselor. If I let myself go, I would experience the fivefold temptations experienced by Elijah. Men under stress face temptations that seem too much to bear: depression, despair, resignation, failure and inferiority.

Nancy's comment caught me, though. Instantly deflated from my tension, I sank into a kitchen chair and willingly let her minister to me. The conference would be great. The ministry was going well. The kids had each been through the same thing before and were capable of overcoming all. The board meeting was in God's hands. My friend could wait until next week. The book would get written, and why don't we just let ourselves relax and enjoy our guest for a few hours. What a relief!

Change is normal to life, and stress is normal to change. Stress is normal to life.

America's forefathers lived in stress. Fighting to be free from political tyranny, opening new frontiers in an ever-expanding country, working through tension with Native Americans, using almost primitive transportation and equipment were only some of the anxieties. Major differences between their time and ours are the pace of life, the distance between neighbors and the moral quality of society.

Jesus' authority came, in part, from knowledge of Who He was, His purpose in life and an identity with which He was in perfect agreement.

Our entire world is in transition. Statistics, either positive or negative, point to the stress of change. U.S. business is on the move, with a half million firms relocating to new facilities in 1989. Upheavals accompany such moves, with two-thirds of executives fired, demoted or quitting. The U.S. has experienced a 618 percent increase in births out of wedlock over the last five years. The crime rate has increased 1,050 percent. More than $71 billion is lost annually through drugs, and $33,000 is stolen per addict per year. [1]

Television isn't even relaxing. A recent study "found that the longer a person watched the set, the more drowsy, bored, sad, lonely and hostile he would become."[2] David Frost, the television personality, said, "Television is an invention that permits you to be entertained in your living room by people you wouldn't have in your home."[3]

Office stress follows many home. Reports say 28 percent of all managers bring stress home, but 57 percent say they rarely bring family tensions to work.[4] At the same time, stress in the home is often greater than stress at work. Researchers say that women working outside the home are happier even though stress increases from juggling home and work responsibilities.[5] The hypothesis is that paid employment is an antidote to depression, and work provides a sense of worth women don't receive at home.

Unemployment among men produces the highest levels of stress in every survey. Work problems and financial difficulties are central, not only to male suicides, but also to suicide-homicides. Many men use work to avoid dealing with personal problems. Men work longer hours when they are facing problems, as if by keeping busy, they don't have to feel.

I'm not commenting on right or wrong, just that stress is there.

Concerns for parents come from the insecurity and risk they feel leaving their children in child-care. Finding someone responsible has become a high-risk, high-stress venture for single mothers especially.[6]

Children eat breakfast in the morning, looking at kidnapped or lost children's pictures on milk cartons. Fingerprinting children is commonplace. Date-rape, murder and violence on campuses have brought fear to students and barricades to dormitories. In inner cities, both the young and the aged fear to venture outside their houses due to gang violence, in effect, being held hostage by rampaging youth.

Financial stress is universally felt. Debtor nations are at the mercy of others, but lending nations are beholden to prop up the failing economies of borrowers. Personal debt kills the productivity through which nations became strong. Easy credit allures. High interest credit cards proliferate among unemployed college students in America. College presidents have to battle the crisis created by greed.

Young married couples are encouraged by salesmen, marketers, advertisers and bankers to enter easy payment plans, only to be trapped by usury. Seduced by avarice, they try to obtain in three years what it took their parents thirty years to accumulate. Debt strains and often fractures the relationship. Some recognize temptation for what it is, and others don't.

Financial pressure, like any stress, can drive men to desperation, but it needn't overwhelm the real man. *"You are a poor specimen if you can't stand the pressure of adversity."*[7]

Financial difficulty drove a man to get a loan. The banker told him he might or might not get it.

"Tell you what I'll do," the banker said. "I have one good eye and one glass eye. Tell me which one is the glass eye, and I'll give you the loan."

The man looked carefully and long into the banker's eyes and then said, "The right eye."

"How did you know?" asked the startled banker.

"Because I thought I saw a little mercy in that eye," the man answered.

CHRISTLIKENESS RESOLVES STRESS

Jesus was without personal stress in Himself, though He bore the sins of the world. Only doing what He saw the Father do relieved Him from the pressure of having to perform on His own. He had the backing of Heaven for all He did.[8] Regardless of the turmoil around Him, He was without insecurity. Neither was He insecure in His identity. His open confession of Himself came from His established heart.[9] Spoken with

Financial pressure, like any stress, can drive men to desperation, but it needn't overwhelm the real man.

perfect equanimity, His testimony was attested by His deeds. "Believe me for what I say, or believe for my work's sake," He said.[10]

He never manipulated, threatened or gave ultimatums. He spoke "as one having authority, and not as the scribes."[11] Jesus' authority came, in part, from knowledge of Who He was, His purpose in life and an identity with which He was in perfect agreement.

Real men are Christlike. Secure in their identification with Jesus, acting in faith on God's Word, believing God will perform what He says, they move through life's trials and circumstances with confidence and face adversity with courage.

Pressure is normal and even needed in life. The right amount of tension in a guitar or piano string is necessary for fine tuning. Too much and it will snap. Water, steam and ice are made from the same substance, as are carbon, graphite and diamonds. It's the pressure that makes the difference. *The more pressure matter is able to withstand, the more valuable it becomes.*

It's the same with people. I'll never forget a pastor friend in Florida who was undergoing pressure that seemed unbearable. A godly man, desiring to do the right thing in the midst of much wrong, he struggled to maintain his personal equilibrium, to minister in love and grace and to determine the will of God for his life and congregation.

During that time, he found these positive aspects of stress which I've never forgotten:

- Stress is necessary for spiritual growth.[12]
- Stress produces more love in committed people.[13]
- Stress produces a greater degree of sanctification.[14]
- Testing prepares you for greater works.[15]
- Stress causes the greatest need for prayer.[16]
- Stress comes from resisting Satan.[17]
- Testing comes before victory.[18]
- Stress produces seeking after God, and that glorifies Him.[19]

Stress is not a new phenomenon. Everyone in every generation has faced his own peculiar pressures. Leadership always has it. The greater the responsibility, the greater the pressure.

But God was the phrase that changed Joseph's life centuries earlier.[20] Sold down the river, falsely accused and jailed, Joseph never lost faith in God. God eventually elevated him to the highest position in government. *What men meant for evil, God meant for good in Joseph's life.*

All trials and temptations end positively if committed to God. God always starts on the positive and ends on the positive. It is the nature of God to change things in our lives for the good. There is pressure in change, but change is the only constant in maturity.

All that is stressful in your life today has the potential for good or for harm. Determine to be changed through the refining fire of pressure, believe God to enable you to overcome the fivefold temptations, lose yourself in identity with Jesus Christ, seek His wisdom in the critical decisions and let stress work for the good to make you a stronger man.

18

Peace for All Seasons

THE FRIGATE GENTLY ROLLED, BARELY VISIBLE on the ocean, with the early morning clouds just lifting over its stacks. From the deck, my shipmates and I could see the destroyers and cruisers we supported looming large in the distance. With the lifting fog, we could make out tiny moving specks which were the Navy crewmen on deck.

Suddenly, Japanese bombers screamed through the clearing sky and began dropping their payloads. The sailors swung into action, bombarding the air with rounds of ammunition. The bombers circled and returned. Out of their ranks came the kamikaze attackers, diving headlong to sink our ships by destroying their planes.

I stood awestruck, stunned, on the deck of the frigate. My shipmates and I had been at sea for an entire year doing convoy and escort duty without ever touching land, but this was the fiercest and closest action we'd seen. We had only a three-inch and some 40mm and 20mm guns with which to defend ourselves, and all guns were firing.

We watched spellbound as the battle unfolded. The smell of burning oil, exploding ammunition and stench from the beach putrefied the salty air. Screaming planes, booming guns and exploding bombs overpowered our ears until all we heard was rumbling. I looked up after a few minutes, which felt like hours, and saw a Japanese plane heading straight for our deck.

If I had been stunned before, now I was frozen. I had not lived for God in years, but I called on Him like He was my best friend. I promised I'd serve Him if He got me out of this.

I stared in disbelief at what was surely to be the last thing I would see on this earth.

Suddenly, the kamikaze plane dove into the ocean and exploded, just missing us. Through the smoke, I could barely see pieces floating on the water. It was gone. Vanished. My attention fell back to the ships, but the battle was ending.

The calm of the ocean returned. The men on the destroyers cleaned up, took care of the wounded, put out fires, rebuilding to prepare for the next battle.

Months later, when I was finally home, peace was eminent. I knew I wouldn't be back at sea again, because the war was ending. When I went home to discuss my plans with my mother, she asked me about the battle I had experienced. It was etched in my mind, and I'd had months to relive it. I told her about it in vivid detail. When I described the kamikaze plane exploding, she shrieked, "That was it!"

She had been lying in bed sleeping that same day when suddenly she sat upright and cried, "My son!" She didn't know what awakened her, but she prayed fervently, beseeching God's protection in my behalf, interceding with Him to rescue me, believing for a miracle. God heard my mother's prayers.

I learned two things in that war. The power of prayer. And, peace is worth fighting for. Peace comes from victory.

In 1988, I was in England when Mr. Reagan and Mr. Gorbachev signed their historic treaty. One of England's cynical newspapers ran the story with the headline "Western Munich" and a picture of Mr. Chamberlain and Adolph Hitler signing the old, broken treaty at Munich before World War II. Mr. Chamberlain was deceived into believing Hitler's promise of peace because he wanted so desperately to avoid war.

The newspaper's sarcasm showed disbelief of any negotiated peace treaty signed by a Communist leader. For good reason. Dimitry Manuilski, an

Victory requires decisiveness in leaders, ruthlessness in discipline and willingness to fight until the battle is over and the victory is won.

instructor at the Lenin School of Political Warfare in Moscow, wrote in 1930 about Communism's plan to defeat the free world: "We shall begin by launching the most spectacular peace movement on record. There shall be electrifying overtures and unheard-of confessions. As soon as their guard is down, we will smash them with our clenched fist."[1]

During the Reagan-Gorbachev summit, twenty-five wars raged in various parts of the world. Of them, only one was between nations. The others were fought within countries, faction against faction, brother against brother. A research institute provided these shocking statistics: "Since the end of World War II in 1945, the death total in wars, rebellions and uprisings of various sorts have taken the lives of 17 million people."[2]

PEACE COMES FROM THE HEART

According to the Bible, peace will not come through treaties, summit conferences or negotiated settlements as long as men have war in their hearts. The state of the heart is at fault, not just the politics involved.

David, king of Israel, had a trusted friend and advisor named Ahithophel,[3] who possessed great wisdom and stood as a spokesman for God. David relied on him. When David's son, Absalom, tried to steal the kingdom, Ahithophel defected to serve Absalom.[4] Knowing that Ahithophel's advice to Absalom could defeat him, David sent another trusted counselor to confound the wisdom of Ahithophel. The counselor posed as a defector also and convinced Absalom to undermine the advice of Ahithophel. David's strategy succeeded. Absalom was defeated and killed, and Ahithophel committed suicide.[5]

David was heartbroken at what happened. He mourned his son, but also lamented the loss of his friend, grieved over the betrayal. David wrote,

For it is not an enemy who reproaches me;
Then I could bear it.
Nor is it one who hates me who has magnified himself
against me;

Then I could hide myself from him.
But it was you, a man my equal,
My companion and my acquaintance.
We took sweet counsel together,
And walked to the house of God in the throng.[6]

Later he said of Ahithophel:
The words of his mouth were smoother than butter,
But war was in his heart;
His words were softer than oil,
Yet they were drawn swords.[7]

There is no peace with men who have war in their hearts.

The angels knew this when they pronounced Christ's birth, saying, "And on earth peace among men with whom He is well pleased."[8] The correct translation is peace "among men" not "toward men." Peace can be found only in men whose hearts are filled with the good will of God, with His love shed abroad in them, and concern for the well-being of others.

Whether it is in marriage, business, civic enterprise, religion, social intercourse, there is no peace where war is in the heart.

Peace comes from the heart, not the peace table.

Real peace comes after total victory. Little or no peace comes from a negotiated compromise. America found this to be true through two different wars. World War II was a "soldiers' war." Military leaders Eisenhower, MacArthur, Bradley, Patton, Nimitz and Marshall led men into battle to win a victory. Our enemies were defeated and relegated themselves to peaceful pursuits. The victors reveled in it. The Allied Forces went home in glory and honor, lauded and decorated.

Men who live by conviction are "strong." Men who live by convenience are "weak."

Vietnam, on the other hand, was a "politicians' war." Major decisions were made by committee through compromise. Soldiers resisted the politicians' tactics and argued for more battlefield efficiency, but "political expediency" prevailed. America's policy makers finally settled for a truce. When the troops came home, they suffered reproach, were looked at with disdain and even spat upon. To this day, some suffer, not only from the war, but from the rejection on their return.

The soldiers were fighting for victory. The politicians were negotiating for compromise. Without victory, people wanted someone to blame. The soldiers bore the brunt of it. I've had men's meetings where Vietnam veterans stood just so the rest of us could cheer them and say, "Thank you!" They fought for our country. They deserve our appreciation. God bless them.

Victory requires decisiveness in leaders, ruthlessness in discipline and willingness to fight until the battle is over and the victory is won.

On the way to Calvary, Satan tempted Jesus to accept reward without paying the price.[9] This devilish temptation to compromise was an opportunity to avoid the ignominy of the Cross, with its humiliation, shame and agony. Jesus refused. He knew: *No cross, no crown!*

The Cross became the place of defeat for Satan and victory for Jesus and all who would trust Him. Having defeated Satan, obtained the peace of His victory, Jesus can now offer His Peace to those who believe and receive Him. "Peace I leave with you, My peace I give to you; not as the world gives do I give to you."[10]

DON'T MAKE A TRUCE WITH SIN

The peace this world offers is ephemeral, transitory and without eternal substance, rooted in a nature that is at enmity with God. Peace that Christ gives is the grounds for the security, safety, prosperity and happiness for men everywhere.

Christ's peace is issued in the spirit. Its moral effect is not just an absence from guilt, but a clear conscience, quiet rest for the soul, an internal harmony in the spirit and a beneficent relationship with fellow human beings. Trust in Christ brings rest to the spirit.

The causes of war in men's hearts are varied:

- The flesh lusts against the spirit.[11] Lusts war in the members.[12]
- Time constraints overwhelm us. Men who compromise with time are "lazy." Men who conquer time are "productive."
- Convictions defect to convenience. Men who live by conviction are "strong." Men who live by convenience are "weak."

A Tulsa man had wrestled with pornography throughout his life, from his early teens to his present thirties. No amount of Christian counsel or prayer seemed to help. One Friday, as he planned his indulgences while his wife was away for the weekend, he remembered my words from a meeting he'd attended: "I will not compromise."

"I fell flat on my face and cried out to God, confessing my sins," he wrote later. "The words *I will not compromise* kept running through my mind. I took index cards and wrote it on them. I put them on the mirror where I shave, the refrigerator, the dashboard of my car. With the continual help of God and the prayers of others, those four words became a reality in my life."

The presence of God cannot be separated from the power of God. To the degree men yield to temptations, there is a loss of both peace and power.[13] The devil's playground is the defeated soul.

Fighting for victory is difficult, but the fight is far easier than the consequences of truce-making with besetting sins.

What is yielded to grows stronger, while what is resisted grows weaker.[14]

Such power, liberty, peace and joy come from the Cross! Jesus Christ said, "My yoke is easy, and my burden is light."[15] Men yoked to lies, fraud, addictions, thievery, vanity or arrogance carry a heavy burden. Men yoked to truth, honesty, love, repentance and faith carry light burdens. Only a fool would not exchange bondage for liberty.

Fighting for victory is difficult, but the fight is far easier than the consequences of truce-making with besetting sins. One of the properties of discipline in the life of Jesus Christ was His ruthlessness.

"If your eye causes you to sin, pluck it out!" He said. "If your hand or foot causes you to sin, cut it off and cast it from you."[16]

"A righteous man who falters before the wicked is like a murky spring and a polluted well."[17]

Jesus Christ had a ruthless attitude toward sin, manifested in His dedication to eradicate it. Men who would be Christlike cannot afford to play "footsie" with Satan or sin. Ruthlessness with self is necessary to excise sin and Satan from life.

Joshua learned well the misery of compromise after becoming leader of Israel. God's "scorched earth" policy was to keep the Israelites from subscribing to foreign gods. God told Joshua to totally defeat every nation in the land He gave them. God said He would make the Israelites conquerors.

In Israel's triumphant march into Canaan, the resident nations cringed in terror. The Gibeonites feared Israel. Rather than fight Israel, they devised a scheme to deceive Joshua into making a truce. Wearing ragged clothes and carrying moldy bread, they met Joshua, claiming to be from a distant land, though they lived in Canaan. Joshua fell for their ruse. He offered them fresh provisions and exchanged a peace treaty with them. Joshua discovered their duplicity too late. He could not violate the treaty and had to surrender that part of the "Promised Land." As a result, the Gibeonites became a snare to the entire nation of Israel.[18]

Much of the misery of life can generally be traced to a truce with sin.

Agreement is one means of obtaining peace. The place of agreement is the place of power. The place of disagreement is the place of powerlessness.

This truth is valid personally and nationally. Until the Gulf War, America suffered from the chasm that developed during Vietnam. In World War II, the nation was united. In Vietnam, it was divided. The Bible teaches, "A kingdom divided against itself is brought to desolation, and a house divided against a house falls."[19]

Disunity killed America's initiative during Vietnam, and the schism led to compromise and truce. A truce in war is like a tie in football—nobody wins. Unity, however, generates power to any person or group of people. America underwent another crisis called "Watergate." The country reeled under the weight of shame, slander, scandal, accusations and a breakdown of trust mistrust. One deeply involved man testified on TV, "We didn't start out as criminals. We were just men who compromised our convictions, and one thing led to another."

One thing held the nation together: the Constitution of the United States. The country was in agreement that the Constitution must be upheld. Agreement upon the written word saved the nation.

In the same way, agreement with the Word of God will save a man from compromise, and make for peace. "Unite my heart to fear Your name," was the cry of the Psalmist.[20] Scripture exhorts to "pursue the things that make for peace,"[21] and an established heart united in one purpose makes for peace.

CHOICES DETERMINE DESTINY

We wrestle between forces—godly, devilish and fleshly—constantly. In the tensions of a life, wrestling between choices of family and profession, recreation and work, ethics and cheating, church and pleasure, when the choice is made to obey God's Word, the result is peace—harmony with God, self, and others. *Submission to the godly brings resistance to the devilish and power over the flesh.*

The Apostle Paul said, "All things are lawful for me, but I will not be brought under the power of any."[22] And, "Do you not know that to whom you present yourselves slaves to obey, you are that one's slaves whom you obey, whether of sin to death, or of obedience to righteousness?"[23]

Everything in life is under our power of choice, but once the choice is made, we become the servant to the choice.

The choice of drug use makes a slave of substance abusers. Dropping out of school produces paupers indentured to ignorance and the limitations it brings. Our choice of a marriage partner can make a rich, rewarding life or a poor existence. Submission to patience is the key to finding the right woman. Selecting the right food and opting for exercise will serve the body well so it can be worn in good health. Enjoying the disciplines of study and developing powers of concentration serve knowledge, which translates into authority.

Choices determine destiny.

Abraham made a wrong decision, and the entire world was affected. Childless at the age of eighty-six, he followed Sarah's advice to impregnate her maid, Hagar. Hagar bore Ishmael. Realizing his error, Abraham decided to trust God for Sarah to conceive a child. God was faithful and gave them Isaac, the child of promise.[24] But the result of Abraham's defection from faith, making a decision after the flesh and not the spirit, is the enmity between the descendants of Sarah and Hagar—the Jews and the Arabs.[25]

Once you choose, you become the servant of that choice. A public school administrator in Maryland used this statement as personal motivation. Over the years, he had gained about seventy pounds. He looked at a sandwich and chips the day after hearing this and said, "Sandwich and chips, if I eat you, I'm going to be a slave to you!" He enrolled in a weight-loss program that week, lost the weight, has kept it off for two years, and enjoys peace of heart and mind. Making the right choice led to peace.

Look at the facets of peace:

- There is a "rest" that comes from God. It overcomes anxiety.[26]

- There is a contentment that God gives. It overcomes restlessness.[27]
- There is a sense of having found something with God. It overcomes searching.[28]
- There is a sense of peace and security with God. It overcomes strife.[29]

God is not the author of confusion.[30] He has made provision for peace through Christ. Jesus is called the "Prince of Peace."[31] He promises to give us peace.[32] "Peace is the umpire for knowing the will of God.[33]

His message is a word of peace.[34] A word of wisdom from the Holy Spirit brought peace to the early Church when they were at an impasse.[35]

Jesus held His peace.[36] Men lose their peace by opening their mouths when they should keep them shut. A raging fire is made from a little kindling. One word spoken at the wrong time can start an argument that ends in tragedy.

The truest, fullest peace comes through Christ, knowing that He fought and won the peace. It is wonderful to know that by His indwelling Spirit in us, He will bring His victory and peace in our lives.

Jesus looked over Jerusalem and wept because they did not recognize the hour of their visitation from God. "Would that you had known personally," He said, "even at least in this your day, the things that make for peace"—freedom from the distress that results from sin, and upon which peace depends.[37]

Don't make the mistake and not recognize the hour of your visitation from God. Achieve peace through Christ. Have this quality of life in which the real man enjoys a full sense of security, safety, prosperity and happiness.

19

Leadership That Works

LEADERS ARE MADE, NOT BORN. MEN WERE born with an "ego mastery" to equip them for leadership. The capabilities of leadership are inherent in the nature of every man.

Three distinguishing characteristics of popular leaders are:

- *Uninhibited in lifestyle*—identifying with purposes and goals without thought to self
- *Fervent in spirit*—likened to the contagion in disease that is found only when fever is present
- *Zealous*—the ardent, impassioned and persevering desire of a cause or purposeful pursuit in life

One of these is enough to command a following. Any two can make a musician a star or create a political movement from a simple boycott. All three found in one man can change the course of history.

Winston Churchill, a stouthearted leader during World War II, rallied his nation through influence gained by his ability to communicate. His speeches are still studied as models for students who desire to lead. Mr. Churchill is said to have possessed nerve and verve, chilling determination, words of resolve (positive and potent), certitude of rightness in his moral compass and implacable courage. Uninhibited in lifestyle, fervent in spirit and zealous for his cause, he commanded a following not only in his own nation but in others as well, and helped defeat Adolph Hitler's mad designs for this world.

Jesus Christ is the epitome of leadership characteristics, the source of their origination and the ultimate expression of them in ministry. He was uninhibited in His lifestyle, being totally identified with the Father.[1] His fervency was exhibited in His diligent application to the Father's will.[2] And His zeal for the Father's house was evident not only when He drove the moneychangers out of the tempole,[3] but also in the surrender of His life. Men followed Him, devoted themselves to Him and gave themselves over to His cause. Real men still do.

Christ fulfilled these three dynamic characteristics and the six qualifications God requires for true leadership.

Paul, under the influence of the Holy Spirit, listed for Timothy a catalog for church bishops that is applicable to men in leadership today. A leader is to be blameless, the husband of one wife, temperate, sober-minded, of good behavior, hospitable, able to teach, not given to wine, not violent, not greedy for money, gentle, not quarrelsome, not covetous, one who rules his own house well, having his children in submission with all reverence, not a novice, and of good reputation.[4]

These qualifications fall under the headings of reputation, ethics, morality, temperament, habits and maturity.

REPUTATION

A man's reputation is seen in the regard given his name. "A good name is to be chosen rather than great riches."[5] A man's reputation is established by the esteem, respect and honor given. Real men recognize the importance of their reputation among peers and with their wives and children.

> The real man values his stature with his family more than the regard of his peers.

One of my heroes is a New Orleans man who changed his entire life for the sake of his family. It began when his sons were arrested for a second time, and he determined to find out what was going on. By questioning them, he found that his good reputation among peers, employees, his church and others was not shared by his own sons.

Others thought he was energetic about the Lord's business and successful. They held him in high regard. His sons thought he was more interested in other things than in them, that he was willing to sacrifice them on the altar of his fame, and they resented Jesus for taking their dad's time and energy.

Shocked and startled, he realized he needed to do something to repair the damage done by his zealousness. *Moses in his zeal killed an Egyptian. This man in his zeal was destroying his relationship with his sons.*

He took a leave of absence from work and spent time with his family, lavishing attention on his sons, praying over every detail of their lives. Months later, he stood before a group of men and told of the wonderful new relations he had with his family. He had finally gained a good reputation with his children.

This man understood the necessity of qualifying for his leadership position. The real man values his stature with his family more than the regard of his peers.

ETHICS

Ethics is more than a study for college students who major in philosophy. Ethics provide a guideline to relationships in business, marriage or even crime. Criminals have a code of what they consider to be ethical conduct. If someone violates it, he is expendable.

A study reported that the new generation has little or no understanding of ethics and little or no desire to study or be guided by ethics. They consider ethics to be archaic posturing, without merit for modern men. Perhaps this is due to the lack of ethics in home life. Sibling rivalry is common when parental ethics are violated by showing favoritism among the children. *Ethical behavior by parents in regard to children is necessary to balanced relationships.*

In business and government, however, the study of ethics is booming. It is the new cry of responsible adults. What has made ethics so "hot" are things like insider trading on Wall Street. Lawyers plead for leniency based on the good that clients have done for society and ask the court to ignore the near total wreckage of businesses, the loss of billions of dollars, and the heavy burden taxpayers will have to bear for years.

A lack of ethics blinds men to their own wrong-doing. The lack of ethics in the governments of many nations is the cause of their chaos and destruction. National ethics in America can be traced to the application of biblical principles. Where moral absolutes are missing in individuals, families or nations, there is no foundation for ethical behavior.

Immoral "religious" ethics are represented in the New Testament by the Pharisees and Sadducees. Pharisees were the legalists who took things that were relative and made them absolutes. Sadducees are those who took absolutes and made them relative. Both secular and sacred "Pharisees" today do the same.

MORALITY

Morality is a system of ethical conduct, relating to principles of right and wrong behavior. Morality can be called "virtue." *Virtue,* in one sense, is used in the Bible synonymously with *courage.*

Moral cowardice is the bane of manhood, moral courage its virtue.

Morality is more than "yes" and "no," good and bad. The immorality of wasting life, failing to do right and making poor decisions goes beyond the morality we fight for in keeping ourselves pure from lust, compromise and common moral failures.

Mike Singletary, the great all-pro football linebacker from the Chicago Bears, invited me to his hometown one evening to speak to some friends and teammates. Upon arrival, I found he had rented a hotel auditorium and invited a great number of people for the evening. I was, and am, deeply impressed by his moral courage and the importance he placed on ministering to those around him.

"Here's a guy who I think has something to say," he told them. "My friend, Ed Cole." Then he sat down, as eloquent an introduction as was needed. I talked to his friends about the five reasons we need courage: We need courage to face reality, admit need, confess wrong, change, make decisions and hold convictions.

Many men will exhibit courage on the football field or in their professions but balk at exhibiting moral courage in the locker room among the profane, at home in making decisions or in attending church on the weekend. As a result, they become cowardly toward Christ.

Men often fail to qualify for leadership because of moral cowardice.

Moral cowardice leads some men to relinquish leadership because of intimidation. My friend Hal was responsible for leading a large group of men in his city and had to deal with men of renown, wealth, power and prestige, but he felt intimidated. Never having had the kind of success these men enjoyed, Hal's feelings of inferiority troubled him and caused him to doubt his leadership. His pastor and I prayed for him. With incomparable wisdom, the pastor prayed what became a healing word for Hal. "Lord, teach Hal that he does not have to be a peer with men he is called to serve."

The statement relieved Hal of insecurity and inferiority and gave him confidence in leadership. Many pastors who serve prominent, successful men are intimated and unable to meet their needs because of a sense of inferiority, so they settle for mediocrity. In that prayer was wisdom for pastors and an antidote to moral cowardice.

We often look for morality in the way of temperance and sexual purity,

We need courage to face reality, admit need, confess wrong, change, make decisions and hold convictions.

but God looks for even more. Moral courage qualifies men to be leaders of those they esteem to be greater than themselves.

During a visit to the U.S. Naval Academy, Secretary of the Navy James H. Webb, Jr., addressed the men and women of the Brigade of Midshipmen, saying:

> A true leader must set the example. You cannot ask of your subordinates that which you do not demand of yourself. The best leaders make decisions, have a clear sense of mission and express it. They have the courage to do what is right and to make sure that those who are under their authority do the same. Courage, both moral and physical, is a character trait that can infect others.[6]

TEMPERAMENT

Richard told me about the time he was selling his businesses to a large, powerful company. In discussing the sale and its terms, the New York lawyers attempted to intimidate Richard, his partner and their hometown lawyers. Imposing, manipulating, exploiting, the big-time lawyers tried everything to wring concessions out of them, take all they could and leave them with as little as possible.

Richard refused to be badgered, goaded into anger or cowed into subservience. He depended on the temperament God had given him through years of renewing his mind with the Word of God and becoming a new creature in heart, soul and emotions.

"I finally told them they needed me more than I needed them," Richard said. "I gave them my terms, take it or leave it. We went through a year of negotiations before it was done, but in the end, I won."

Richard's boldness and firmness were based on knowing who he was in God and that he didn't have to be bullied or beaten by anybody. Men who browbeat mock those who are beaten. Richard was neither.

A temperate man doesn't make decisions based on the emotion of the moment or on the personal gratification he can garner but on the merits of the decision itself. The real man's criteria for decision making are: Is it spiritual, moral, ethical, legal? Holding to that standard, refusing to be swayed, keeping personal feelings in hand makes for good leadership.

HABITS

Physical habits find their roots in mental traits. How a man thinks, his secret thought patterns, are basic to habitual behavior. Actions follow beliefs. Emotions follow actions. *Change a mind, change a habit, change a life.*

When Israel entered the Promised Land, the people were told to destroy Canaan's idols and images, so idolatry would not become a snare to them. The leaders assisted in tearing down the great idols in the cities, but winked at the "high places" in the land and allowed the people to worship at them.[7] The high places represented places they retreated to in secrecy to worship false gods. Eventually the high places led to the official reinstitution of idolatry.

The high places in men's minds are secret thoughts—strongholds of nostalgia, sentiment or fantasy, to name a few. Men retreat into these to satisfy their natural desires. Creative mental habits are constructive, compulsions and obsessions are destructive. Fantasizing through pornography seems, at first, to be a non-hazardous occupation—merely going to some high place for a few moments of recreational worship to an image created in the mind. But when it finds its release, it can lead to incest, rape, homosexuality and deadly diseases.

God's "scorched earth policy" regarding idolatry is to tear down idols—"high places" and all.

Sons who are unwilling to forgive their fathers, who grudge against their sins, find pleasure in thinking of ways

> A temperate man doesn't make decisions based on the emotion of the moment or on the personal gratification he can garner but on the merits of the decision itself.

to hurt their dads. "High place" imaginations that worship the idols of hatred and vengeance hold sway. Such habits of the mind must not be tolerated in any man's life. They can lead to despicable actions.

Habitually washing the mind with the water of the Word of God,[8] practicing positive prayers, repetitively quoting Scripture, methodically and systematically reading the Bible and routinely worshipping all develop godly traits, build character and give quality to life.

We are creatures of habit. *Habits can be developed by default or determination.*

Perhaps the greatest man I have ever known (who, because of humility, won't permit me to use his name) arrived at his stature as a world leader by choosing to read at least one great book every week of his life. Over the last thirty years, he has read more than two thousand of the greatest books ever written. People wonder why he is where he is. Because books, not dogs, are a man's best friend. Good habits are his friends, too.

MATURITY

The marks of a mature man can be seen in a variety of ways: the facets of character, friends he chooses, decisions he makes, responsibility he accepts, leadership he exercises and so on.

Leaders are men who determine to influence, followers only happen to influence.

Leaders are those who set the example, are decisive, have a clear sense of mission, show courage, accept accountability, understand true loyalty, get the job done, take care of their people, are able to motivate others, are able to communicate properly and are content to be themselves.

In 1987, in Harare, Zimbabwe, three ladies had what they called "a word from God." Tight scheduling prevented me from meeting with them, but the ex-police chief inspector coordinating our men's meetings in that country became the mediator to give me their message. Being a former military officer, he first gave me the background. Rhodesia was at war for fourteen years until it became Zimbabwe. During the war, the men spent six weeks in the bush fighting, then six weeks at home working. The tension and anxiety in the home and nation was incredible.

Godly women engaged in intercessory prayer for their men and nation. They began to see themselves as "Esthers." The Bible records Esther as a queen who interceded for her people and nation before the king. An edict was given to annihilate her race of people in the king's country. When her uncle discovered the terrible plot, he exhorted her to boldness, saying, "Who knows whether you have come to the kingdom for such a time as this?"[9]

Praying Rhodesian women believed they had come to their nation for such a time as this civil war. The war ended. Rhodesia became Zimbabwe. The men came home. But now something new required their intercession as much as before. The men had become passive, complacent and lethargic. "Esthers" saw the need for intercession in peacetime as much as in wartime.

For seven more years, they continued uninterrupted intercession. One day in prayer, these ladies were impressed with a "word" for the men of their nation. They held it, laying it up "for an appointed time."[10] A year later, they heard the teaching that "manhood and Christlikeness are synonymous." They believed the "word" they had was for me and the men's ministry.

It was so simple, that, at first, I almost dismissed it, but it grew in my spirit until I came to believe it is a word for men, not only of Zimbabwe, but for this entire generation—for men who have let the women take the leadership role in the church, home and nation.

The word is: "There was a time for Esthers, but today is a time for Daniels."

Powerful!

> Now is the time for men to accept the spiritual and moral leadership of the home, church and community.

These women had to bear the burden in the heat of the day. They bore the responsibilities men dropped when they vacated their places of leadership and remained absent from them after returning home. "Esthers" saw it as pertaining to their nation. I saw it as pertaining to men the world over.

Now is the time for men to accept the spiritual and moral leadership of the home, church and community. This is a call from God, not just women, for men to be like Daniels in this present world—leaders in home, church and country.

Today is a day for Daniels. God speaks to you to cast down the "high places" and become concerned about the six characteristics that qualify you to be His leader. *First and foremost, every real man establishes his relationship to God.*

The real man approaches every day conscientiously living out the characteristics that qualify him to become a leader—the leader God created him to be.

Part 6

Real Roles

The Irresistible Husband

FROM THE BAYOU COUNTRY OF LOUISIANA COMES a story of Cajun humor.

"Wha's dat unna yo shirt?" a friend asks.

"It's the dyn-o-mite ah've strapped to mah chest," replies the man.

"Why you got dyn-o-mite tied ta yo chest?" the friend inquires.

"You know how Louis always come up to me and poke me inna chest all the time? Well, dah next time he poke me inna chest, I gonna blow his han'off!"

Trying to remedy an annoying situation was going to cause him more harm than good. We can do the same in marriage. A husband may try to correct situations in his marriage without using wisdom or understanding and alienate himself further from his wife and family.

On a recent television talk show, women vented their anger toward their mates and dates. In one thirty-minute segment, remarks such as these erupted: "All men are jerks;" "He was more boy than man;" "All men live by their primal passions." These comments represent what many women feel today.

Most men do not understand that a life devoid of the Spirit of Christ, lacking His grace, is coarse, whereas Spirit-filled righteousness refines character.

Sin desensitizes emotions and concern for others. The Holy Spirit brings sensitivity to others' needs, hurts and desires.

The very nature of God is to work for the good of others. That servant's heart is best exhibited in Jesus—the servant Savior for all.

The same Spirit Who empowered Jesus works in us to:

- create a servant's heart
- augment natural talent
- maximize personality
- highlight awareness of people's needs and desires
- give insight into life's meaning
- deepen understanding
- sharpen and clarify issues

The Spirit is a perfect gentleman, granting us the virtues of gentlemanliness, the fruit of the Spirit—"love, joy, peace, patience, kindness, goodness, faithfulness, gentleness and self-control."[1] *The same virtues are also characteristics of ladylikeness, for they are without gender.*

By contrast, the "works of the flesh" are sins of uncontrolled sensual passion, superstition, social disorder and excess.[2] These scour the mind, soul and body.

What does this have to do with marriage? God, the ultimate gentleman, is in the business of making gentlemen out of husbands. The dissolution of many marriages is caused by the absence of gentlemanly qualities among husbands. Men need the Spirit to do His work in their lives.

The characteristics of a gentleman display themselves in commonplace things like appearance, manners, speech, hygiene, habits and character traits.

Many husbands expect wives to compete with movie "sex goddesses," while exempting themselves from such comparisons with other men. Although neither men nor women need to strive for unrealistic perfection, men can take strides toward self-improvement. Failure to take care of appearance and attire can cause a husband to lose his wife's respect. Neglected hygiene repulses women. Men whose speech is profane, filled with slang, off-color humor, limited vocabulary and willful ignorance bar themselves from more intimate relationships.

In short, husbands who are indifferent to the characteristics of a gentleman diminish their stature, especially to wives. An amazing percentage of complaints I receive in the mail from women deal with a man's indifference to life's common courtesies.

"Let each esteem others better than himself" [3] is a biblical bidding for courtesy. If a man reads the Bible for no other reason than to find a blueprint for a gentlemanly lifestyle, it would be a rewarding experience. Just following the exhortations to courteousness, refinement and respect for others will lead to gentlemanliness. Look at the fruit of a gentlemanly nature.

Gentleness is a sign of strength, not weakness. A man who knows his strength can afford to be gentle. The stronger the man is, the gentler he can be. Insecure men compensate for their lack by abusing others. Putting someone down doesn't build anyone up. King David, with his powerful war record, great riches and reputation, wrote of his relationship with God, saying, "Your gentleness has made me great."[4]

Kindness is a virtue that is attractive to women. Men and women were not created as competitors. Women were created to complete men. When men make women compete with them for attention, affection, attachment, they defeat themselves and nature. Having "brotherly affection" is to be considerate and sympathetic toward others.[5] Such kind affection is critical in marriage.

To be fair, some women seem cut from a different cloth today. It still astonishes me to hear women speak of men's "buns" in the aggressive crudeness formerly found mostly in men. Femininity is a woman's "stock in trade," her strength of nature and her glory. Why give it up for competitive conflict?

Humility is not weakness.[6] Humility comes from the Spirit of God. Moses was called the meekest man on earth,[7] but he was far from weak. Moses learned to control his spirit as he was disciplined by God for forty years in the desert before beginning his public ministry. His ministry was confronting and defeating the greatest political figure in his land, then leading about two million Hebrews out of slavery and into the Promised Land. No task for a weak person!

Leadership scares many men, so women bear the burden of male cowardliness. The unwillingness of men to face responsibility forces women into men's roles. In the Church, men have largely abdicated the roles of leadership, forcing women to fill the gap. In the world, women politicians often enjoy more credibility than the men they replace. It is not common to find top social and political spots occupied solely by women.

For years, Houston had the reputation of being a "man's town." Texans to the core, Houstonians were proud of their heritage and lineage. Oil men, cattle barons, media moguls and just plain "good ole boys" gave Houston its male aura. But no more. In Houston, positions occupied by women include the mayor, hospital chief, Chamber of Commerce president, chief of police, university president and school superintendent.[8]

As men step aside from leadership, specifically in the home, they find less fulfillment in life. Forty-eight percent of middle managers in major companies surveyed said their lives seemed "empty and meaningless," despite striving to achieve professional goals. Of senior executives, 68 percent said they had neglected their families, and that, if they could do it over, they would spend more time with their wives and children. Of high achievers, 60 percent felt they had sacrificed their identities to pursue material rewards.[9]

FULFILLING A WIFE'S UNIQUENESS

Recognition of others' uniqueness demonstrates strength. Women were created with a God-given uniqueness.

When that uniqueness is satisfied, she is that man's wife, best friend and the completion of his life. When the uniqueness is ignored, stifled or simply lusted after, she is just another unfulfilled woman.

One woman in exasperation wrote me this letter: "The number one problem in marriage is not lust—it is television. My husband has been involved in church ministry for years, and all our friends have grown in the Lord, but not us. And do you know why? Because he never reads his Bible. He just sits in front of the TV every night while I take care of the children, do the chores, clean the house and get myself ready for work the next day. I wish it would blow up!"

The only thing worse than the wimp, brute or idiot portrayed on the screen is the "Video Daddy" glued to it. Television is a medium of lust. Programs and commercials are full of lust— sexual, material goods, food, "lust for life." Remember, sex was made for loving and giving, not lusting and getting.

A couple told me of the lustful marriage they lived with for years. Jeff was an entrepreneur by nature. They had lived in many different cities, working in many businesses through the years. Everywhere they went, Emily worked side by side with him tirelessly, raising the family as well, tending to their various houses, adapting to new communities and providing him with everything in an attempt to satisfy him.

When the last child finished college, Emily felt herself cool toward Jeff. She was tired. Nothing she had ever done had been quite good enough. She had never worked in their businesses to his satisfaction. Their marriage bed had never left Jeff completely satisfied. Every time Jeff walked past her, he grabbed her sexually.

She avoided him, became irritable and kept him at a distance. As the marriage dissolved, someone gave Jeff a tape on "Love or Lust." Jeff heard more than what was on the tape. He heard God speaking to him.

Weeks later, as Jeff continued in prayer and soul-searching to hear more from God, he took Emily away for the weekend. In the car, he turned on the tape.

"This is the tape that changed my life," he said.

She laughs now that she expected it to be a trick to get her to listen to a message on woman's submission. Instead, she was shocked to hear a confrontational message of truth that nailed Jeff's every flaw. Before the tape ended, Jeff turned it down, leaned toward Emily and asked for forgiveness for thirty years of lusting her, not loving her. In tears, they made a new commitment to each other, and the restoration process began.

Men have appetites and desires, and women have theirs, too. The needs are often met differently, but the basics are the same. In a survey, nearly 50 percent of American wives "cheat" on their husbands in extramarital affairs. This is double the number in 1948. The reasons the wives gave were:

- to force a change in the relationship
- to "prove" their desirability
- to pursue their dream of a "perfect" love
- to relieve boredom and satisfy curiosity
- to take revenge for the husband's known or suspected infidelity, neglect, stinginess, mistreatment of the children, poor personal hygiene

The underlying cause in each is that the woman's uniqueness was not satisfied in the marriage. Her creativity was stifled. Spontaneity was stunted. Sexual overtures were ignored. Romantic inclinations were thwarted.

Some women simply cannot stand the sight of their husbands around the home on the weekends—unshaven, disheveled, loathsome. A good tip written by Abigail Van Buren was: "Don't look like a slob all weekend—unless she looks worse."

It comes back to being a gentleman.

Marriage is the second most important relationship men and women will ever have, and the choice of a mate is the second most important decision they will ever make. The most important is believing on Jesus and building a relationship with God.

The more like Jesus he becomes, the more of a gentleman he will be. Real men are gentlemen. Gentlemen make real marriages.

21

The Fabulous Father

THE LEGACY OF FATHERS IS IN THEIR CHILDREN.
The father is to be the head of the family as Christ is the head of the Church. As such, he must serve his family in the way Christ serves the Church—as prophet, priest and king. As prophet, the father speaks from God to his children. As priest, he speaks for his children to God. As king, he governs, qualifying himself to lead by his willingness to serve them.

Fathers are to be esteemed and respected stewards who are greatly rewarded. Today, however, problems in fatherhood are the direct result of the crisis in manhood. We see men in a spectrum ranging from "Fabulous Fathers" to "Deadly Dads."

America's transition from a producer to a consumer nation has brought a marked change in family mindset. Young people now desire to be satisfied, rather than working to be satisfied. In the "me generation," the goal was to satisfy self. It degenerated into the present solipsism, which is the deifying of self. This philosophy, together with media representations of fathers as a joke, and other profound influences, has produced staggering results.

Children today are often left with just television to raise them. Television is a thief, robbing time, stealing initiative and killing relationships. Most children spend more hours watching

> As prophet, the father speaks from God to his children. As priest, he speaks for his children to God. As king, he governs, qualifying himself to lead by his willingness to serve them.

television than they do in school, leaving little time for rightful role models. Australia, a country that attempts to maintain high standards for their media, reported the average preschooler spends thirty hours per week watching television. Students spent more than 15,000 hours watching television during school years, while receiving 11,000 hours of education. For every seven hours spent watching television, children spent only one hour reading.[1] A cause of low student test scores is poor stewardship of children's time, as television steals more and more of their day.

No wonder teens are in trouble. William Bennett, the former Secretary of Education, voiced this concern:

> Never before has one generation of American teenagers been less healthy, less cared for or less prepared for life than their parents were at the same age. Many—perhaps most—of the problems that worry us are not rooted in institutional bigotry, governmental neglect, societal hardheartedness or disease, but in behavior. And their solutions depend on our willingness to reassert the moral and ethical values of family, community and character.

> Government never raised a child, and it never will. Nothing more powerfully determines a child's behavior than his internal compass, his beliefs, his sense of right and wrong. The character of a society is determined this way; by means of individual morality accruing social capital from generation to generation.[2]

A Los Angeles juvenile court judge said:

> Young people today woefully lack the basic skills of reading, writing, arithmetic. They are illiterates, not because they are ignorant, but because they are educationally handicapped. They are not properly taught, motivated or guided. I have long advocated adding a parenting class to the school curriculum and making it a mandatory requirement for graduation from junior high school and high school.[3]

Speaking from his profession, the same judge quoted a horrible finding: "It is a proven fact that 85 to 90 percent of all delinquent children have been abused, either sexually, emotionally or physically."[4]

When parenting provides only provocation, crooked strokes or abuse, a poor self-image results. Valueless to self, life itself is worthless, so what point is there in living? For those who don't find worth by immoral, illicit or illegal means, suicide becomes an option. Suicide is the second leading cause of death among America's young.

Those who survive teen years are now caught in the backwash of the "baby boom," whose culture and attitudes still dominate American discourse. This generation, in the eighteen-to-twenty-nine bracket, seem almost to be rebelling against rebellion. Apathy and alienation are giving way to disengagement. The findings of two national studies paint a portrait of a generation of these young adults as people indifferent toward public affairs. One reports:

> It is a generation that knows less, cares less, votes less and is less critical of its leaders and institutions than young people in the past ... It is not so much that young adults under thirty are disillusioned, as they are uninterested.[5]

Another study concludes that there is a "citizenship crisis" in which "America's youth are alarmingly ill-prepared to keep democracy alive."[6]

The greatest mission for men today is not to correct what is wrong in adults but to reach and teach what is right to children and youth.

If values and goals are not taught at home, and educational processes deny responsibility for teaching moral values, where will young men and women find them? We must not be

The greatest mission for men today is not to correct what is wrong in adults but to reach and teach what is right to children and youth.

deceived into thinking that institutions, philosophically-adulterated authority figures or media-made role models will teach our children the principles upon which to build not only their lives, but also those of their family and nation. The home is the place where these principles are to be inculcated into the child. The person ultimately responsible is the father. For those without fathers, a fatherly role model from friend or neighbor is vital.

INVEST WHAT YOU'VE LEARNED

Young men must be mentored in the ways of morality, goodness and righteousness. Older men who have found the answer to the world's problems through Christ must focus their efforts on mentoring the young.

Men cannot allow wisdom, experience and knowledge to die with them. They must invest spiritual, physical and material resources entrusted to them and incorporate them into the lives of the young. *Teen-men need to know what real manhood is. They will not find it except in men like you reading this right now.*

Low ambition level, poor self-image, low sociability and emotional deprivation are critical warning signs that an otherwise normal child is becoming liable to abnormal habits or associations.

During the "hippie" generation, when revolutionary-minded students beleaguered and besieged California colleges, when drugs were openly advocated and some professors told collegians to "tune in, turn on and drop out," I served on Governor Reagan's "Council on Children and Youth." Among our responsibilities was to survey rehabilitation units in the state to analyze their effectiveness, to discover who had the lowest rate of recidivism and why.

We were startled to discover that the most successful rehab centers were those which came closest to approximating family life. The more of a "surrogate family" they were, the more successful they became. Teen Challenge had the lowest rate of recidivism among those surveyed.

"Family" means "father's house." Father's problems are sown as seeds into children and reaped as adults. That's why psychologists delve into a patient's childhood (especially the first seven years) to try to find the roots of problems.

One survey listed four basic causes as to why children become vulnerable and susceptible to drugs and alcohol: Low ambition level, poor self-image, low sociability and emotional deprivation are critical warning signs that an otherwise normal child is becoming liable to abnormal habits or associations.

A father's responsibility in the home is to provide intimacy, discipline, love and worth. To the neglected, abused and excluded, cults offer what the home failed to provide: intimacy, discipline, love and worth. Cults thrive on disenfranchised and alienated youths. Interestingly, the same four qualities were provided in the most successful rehab centers surveyed: intimacy, discipline, love and worth.

In his treatise on cults, Bob Larson states that they "demote God, devalue Christ, deify man and denigrate Scripture."[7] But the young respond to their offer of family relationships. Having missed it at home, the cult becomes the substitute family, and the leader or guru is a father figure. Mr. Larson says to combat cults, fathers must teach children:

- the attributes of God
- the person of Christ
- the nature of man
- the requirements of salvation
- the source of all true revelation[8]

These "tenets of faith" cannot be left to some Sunday School teacher, children's church worker, itinerant preacher or pastor. This work is the ministry of the father who is prophet, priest and king in his own home. These tenets are not commonly taught today, as they were in previous generations, because men in the average congregation are untutored in the doctrines themselves and cannot pass them along to their children. Men can give their children only what they possess.

There was a day when fathers in the home were the teachers, and books were the center of family life. Reading to the family in the evening brought culture, attentiveness, quietness and knowledge. It created an image of the father's authority in the family's mind. Often fathers did not have to discipline, but merely spoke, and children obeyed. If children do not learn the work ethic at home, nor how to set and attain short- and long-term goals, aspiration to achieve will be underdeveloped, if not lost altogether.

We are stewards, not owners, of our children. A man's stewardship can never be relinquished. Judgment comes from the measure to which he succeeds.

A father can be both a "Deadly Dad" and a "Fabulous Father" in one home to two different children. King David was a deadly dad to Adonijah but a fabulous father to Solomon. The Bible records that "his father, King David, had never disciplined him [Adonijah] at any time—not so much as by a single scolding."[9] Lack of correction from his father ruined Adonijah. *It is an accepted fact that the quickest way to destroy a child is to give a child anything he wants.*

David prepared for transition by giving his wealth to Solomon to carry out the construction of the Temple and exhorting Solomon to be wise, planting the seed in Solomon's heart that became the basis for requesting wisdom from God. Adonijah rebelled against his father, but Solomon submitted. Adonijah lost his position, but Solomon became king.

Sibling rivalries often have their roots in parental upbringing. Jacob loved Joseph more than his other sons, gifted him with a coat of many colors and created the hostility and jealousy that turned to hatred in the hearts of Joseph's brothers.

Deadly Dads can be doting dads, drinking dads, discordant dads, demanding dads, dividing dads, demeaning dads, defeated dads, departed dads or even demonic dads.

Fabulous Fathers want to see their sons and daughters grow to maturity, be productive, develop normally and enjoy their own families. A man cannot expect to become a "Fabulous Father" by chance. Like anything, good fathering takes study, practice and time. The wise father will take note of what motivates his child through these years and work to channel the energy, not stifle creativity.

God requires fathers: "Do not provoke your children to wrath, but bring them up in the training and admonition of the Lord."[10]

The Apostle John wrote, "I have no greater joy than to hear that my children walk in truth"[11]

A father's primary purpose in parenting is the eternal welfare of his family. It is his responsibility to train his children to live on their own foundation of faith, character and experience, to raise them in the nurture and admonition of the Lord, not to provoke them to wrath and to teach them God's ways so they, in turn, can teach their children.

TEACH YOUR CHILDREN THE COVENANT

Fathers provide teaching and training of righteousness within the home. This includes teaching the sexual sign of the covenant of marriage. The father's honor is to present his children as virgins at their weddings. Teaching a child about his or her sexuality is required earlier and earlier because of the vast amounts of sexual aberrations our society exposes to children. Teaching them, at least in part, before the onset of puberty is critical.

Fathers are to guard against defilement. Physically, fathers guard children from abuse, abortion and addiction. Mentally, fathers guard children from evil reports of all kinds—gossip, films, harshly critical teachers. Spiritually, fathers guard against the attacks of the enemy including discouragement and depression.

Godly fathers need to love as God loves: redemptively, sacrificially and unconditionally. In this same manner a husband is to love his wife as Christ loves the church.

As God loves us, fathers must love their families. A father needs to give his children something that cannot be bought: himself. Toys, no matter how sophisticated, do not replace the person. Nothing impersonal can satisfy the personal. *A Fabulous Father must give his children acceptance, approval, affection, association and a sense of authority.*

A young woman wrote me a pathos-filled letter, encouraging me to continue to minister to men. The reason, she wrote, was that she was born with a physical impediment. Because of it, her father never accepted her. Rejection was all she knew until she found acceptance of her heavenly Father through Jesus Christ. That saved her life.

A sense of association comes from a well-developed sense of belonging. Fathers must make their children feel as though they belong to the family. This is especially true of stepfathers. It's too easy for stepdads to favor their own natural children and withhold the same approval, affection and association from the stepchildren.

Acceptance, approval, affection, association and a sense of authority make a strong foundation. What is built on that foundation is even more directly the father's responsibility, because the healthy child watches and copies his dad. Children learn by example. *It is not the father's responsibility to make all his children's decisions for them but to let them see him make his.*

Children may not always listen to you, but they will always imitate you. This father wrote to me when he found that out:

> One statement that you made, "The character of the kingdom emanates from the character of the king," helped me change as a father. My eldest son, Zachary, nine years old, had been asking me to draw pictures of jet planes for him. He is fascinated by them, likes to read books about them and likes jet toys. Every time he would

ask me to draw for him, I would tell him, "I don't know how, and besides it's too hard." This sequence happened repeatedly with me answering the same way each time.

A few months later, we received a note from his teacher saying that Zachary was not turning in his homework assignments. My wife and I checked his assignments and told him to make sure he turned them in. A few weeks later, we received another note that said he had improved but still was not turning in his homework. I discovered he had done his homework but didn't turn it in. I told him he couldn't play until he turned in his work and asked his teacher to give him make-up work. Again, he didn't turn it in. This time I disciplined him and requested a parent-teacher conference, hoping that God would show me through the conference what the problem was with my son.

I asked the teacher what might be the reason for his behavior. My heart dropped when she said he repeatedly told her, "I don't know how and besides it's too hard."

I remembered another thing you said once, "You'll never beat out of your child what is wrong in your own life." Change had to come first in my own life—so change could happen in my son. I immediately began to draw those jet planes, and my son slowly began to do his homework.

By changing yourself, you can change a multitude of lives around you. Be a Fabulous Father to your children and the fatherless around you. Accept the mission to teach children and teen-men what you have spent a lifetime learning.

Don't bury your legacy of faith when you die. Plant it in some young mind and heart, and let it live long after you're gone. Every son needs a father. Every young man needs a mentor. Deadly Dad or Fabulous Father—you make the choice.

22

The Authentic Friend

AFTER A BROTHERLY GREETING, BRAD AND I settled into chairs, and he began repeating, "It's unbelievable." Years before, Brad stood to make his commitment to Christ in one of our men's events. He became a friend and helped support the ministry. Now alone, in the midst of a divorce, far from home, he and I sat in the privacy of his motel room, and I listened to his tearful story.

Brad had a trusted partner who carried on his business on a daily basis. But this erstwhile, dependable individual did something Brad considered immoral and seditious. When confronted, the man refused to acknowledge wrong, so Brad fired him.

The fired partner then went to work for someone else, took most of Brad's business with him and left Brad mentally confused, emotionally crushed and spiritually debilitated. When the pressure of it reached into Brad's home, his wife did not respond as he thought she should. Overwhelmed, he "opted out." His wife later verified that she had been selfish and didn't support him. Weeping as she spoke of her departed husband, she had pleaded, "Please, Ed, do what you can."

I could do little in that lonely motel room. The best thing, I thought, was to pray with him and be his friend. I put my hand on his should and said, "Brad, I want to be a friend and help you all I can."

Instead of accepting my gesture, he looked up at me sharply.

"I've heard that before!" he said. "What is a friend? Does anyone know how to be a friend? The men I trusted said they were my friends, but they weren't."

His remarks left a sick sense in my gut, like a ten-ton sledge hammer had hit me. The unfaithful, as Brad discovered, are life's greatest hurt.

Faithful friends are life's greatest treasure. Being a true friend is one of the marks of a real man.

Brad's former partner was a traitor. Traitors are not friends, regardless of their professed friendship. In a recent book, the author told of his training as a spy. One experienced spy told him, "Always remember the most important thing: When I am sitting with my friend, he is not sitting with his friend."[1]

A vast difference exists between the men's regard for each other. One is trusting, the other trusts no one. The author explained that, to spies, traitors are the lowest of the low. Yet, he said, "Every agent [spy] is a traitor, no matter how much he rationalizes it."[2]

Judas is regarded with contempt more than pity because he betrayed Jesus. Trusted with the treasury, Judas forgot he was only a steward and not the owner of what he possessed. For the love of money, Judas turned traitor and died an ignominious death.

A man is also not a friend if he advises devious deeds that lead to ruin. In the biblical story of Amnon and Tamar, were it not for a "friend," neither life would have been ruined. Jonadab, who gave Amnon the plan to rape Tamar, was no friend.[3] A true friend would have warned Amnon, rather than advocating and advancing the disastrous scheme.

King David, suffering from Ahithophel's betrayal, wrote, "Even my own familiar friend in

> Faithful friends are life's greatest treasure.
> Being a true friend is one of the marks of a real man.

whom I trusted, who ate my bread, has lifted up his heel against me."[4]

David's words applied to our Lord Jesus when He was betrayed by Judas. Yet Jesus cried on the cross, "Father, forgive them, for they do not know what they do."[5]

Jesus forgave every offense. When we are wounded, hurt or offended by those we regard as friends, those we trust, we cannot allow their feigned faith, hypocrisy or misdeeds to cause us to become bitter and turn against the Lord Who is our only hope. We must die to those things by giving them to the Lord in prayer—trusting Him Who already bore it to heal and sustain us in our trial.

Why walk away from a Friend Who loved us enough to die in our stead that we might have eternal life? Instead of allowing Jesus to give us comfort and assuage our hurts, turning to the "weak and beggarly elements" of the world,[6] we receive only superficial solace and become worse off than ever. What comfort is there in alcohol or drugs? They only deceive us and become our master while promising to serve and give relief. What ease is there from television with its philosophical perversion propagating immorality, that only temporarily salves our bitterness while deepening feelings of anarchy against God? Or the "friendly" woman who provides the "sympathetic shoulder" and open bed, but who creates more distress when she proves as unfaithful as she was to the man she left! There is no healing—only more betrayal and hurt, greater hardening of heart—and what seems good turns out to be evil.

A wife who is a real friend to her husband is a man's greatest protection, source of inspiration and solace.

Jesus is our only refuge! "Do not cast away your confidence, which has great reward."[7] Jesus Himself told us that in this world, we would have tribulation, but to "be of good cheer, I have overcome the world."[8] Peter added that, though the saints' faith would "be tested fire, may [it] be found to praise, honor, and glory at the revelation of Jesus Christ."[9]

I left Brad's room that evening for a meeting with leaders of some men's rallies. Still hurting because of my friend's despair, I asked those leaders, "What is a friend to you?" Their replies were:

- "A friend is someone who knows all my faults and accepts me just as I am."
- "A friend is someone who loves me enough to speak into my life and tell me the truth I need to hear."
- "A friend is someone with whom I can be transparent, vulnerable and honest."
- "The measure of a friend is the degree to which I can share my life with him and not have it come back to me."
- "A friend is someone I can count on in a crisis."
- "A friend to me is like what Jonathan and David had in the Bible."
- "A friend will not leave me or forsake me."

Each answer described Jesus! Jesus is "a friend who sticks closer than a brother."[10] Friendship with Jesus is our greatest hope in times of trouble!

The requirements to be a true friend are greater than to be an acquaintance. Jesus fulfills every one. He said, "No longer do I call you servants ... but I have called you friends."[11] Scripture says, "Faithful are the wounds of a friend."[12] "A friend loves at all times."[13] "Greater love has no one than this, than to lay down one's life for his friends."[14]

We learn how to be friends by studying the friendship of Jesus. True friends are loyal, trustworthy, true and steadfast. Friends help in times of crisis, and the crisis deepens the friendship. The strongest friendships are those forged in the furnace of affliction. To set aside your own concerns in an attempt to resolve another's crisis is a form of dying to yourself. *When it's true friendship, it's done unselfishly with love and devotion.*

When King David was faced with the sedition of Absalom and the defection of his trusted advisor, Ahithophel, God sent another friend, Hushai, to meet David's need. It was the loyalty of a real friend that enabled David to regain his throne.[15] Hushai laid down his life for David and found a firmer friendship with his king. Ahithophel tried to save his life and eventually lost it.[16]

True friends rejoice when their friends do well. Taking joy in another's success provides real fulfillment. My wife is my best friend. She takes great joy in my success and is the greatest contributor to it. A wife who is a real friend to her husband is a man's greatest protection, source of inspiration and solace.

Nancy knows everything about me. The principles of intercession changed our lives. During prayer times together, I became open and vulnerable, able to share my weaknesses with her, knowing she would pray for me—not condemn me. Our relationship was strengthened through the trust developed in friendship.

A wife who is not a real friend has little to offer. Job's wife, in her bitterness, resentment and loss, told her husband to "curse God and die."[17] She was no help in his distress. Neither were the friends who came to mourn and comfort him. Friends are those who speak truth into your life in a time of need, not self-righteous prejudices. To make a friend, you must first be friendly.[18]

Friendship, not romance, holds a marriage together. Friends are life's greatest treasure. Affection between friends can be stronger than love between husband and wife. Jonathan and David had that type of friendship. Scripture describes it as "surpassing the love of women."[19]

Life's greatest commodity is not money but friends. Businessmen need to learn to make friends, not customers. When the clients and customers are gone, friends will still be doing business. Friend-raising rather than fund-raising is the key to longevity because "funds come from friends."

Abraham was called "the friend of God."[20] What greater appellation or accolade can be accorded any man than to have God call him "friend"? God spoke to Moses "face to face, as a man speaks to his friend."[21]

What could be greater than having God call you His friend? Real men need to be friends with other men, with their wives and children and also with Jesus Christ by accepting the friendship He offers.

23

The Greatest Pleasure in Life

NANCY AND I LIKE TO MINISTER IN ENGLAND. We love the British—their humor, Wimbledon and their tea. On a recent trip, I read an article by an Englishman who was complaining about how his countrymen apologize for success. He said success was almost a dirty word in their culture and that great achievements are often followed by an apology for having done so well. The writer traced the attitude to the ancient Greeks. According to him, their philosophy was "Don't get too bumptious, lest you make the gods jealous and they strike you down." He closed his article:

> I'd like to see us shuck off those ancient Greeks and try another God. One who is never jealous, who wants a world where everyone can win at something, which sets high standards but forgives mistakes; a culture where celebration is okay, where joy is part of life and Heaven is still ahead. Of course, it would be quite a revolution.[1]

In the Christian community, we could be given the same ribbing. *Often we act like we're trying to keep from riling God, to pacify Him with good works without sharing in the joy of having done them.*

Scripture states that God is pleased with us. If we accept that, we approach life eagerly, expecting to please Him and freely expressing the joy it brings. Nothing else produces the exuberance, the excitement of pleasing God. There is no need for guilt, embarrassment or shame in attempting to please Him. And there is no mystery in learning how to please Him.

In Washington, D.C., I experienced a day that seemed like a throwback to the old, great church revivals. The Holy Spirit swept over entire auditoriums during those days, calling men to repentance and displaying the glory of the risen Savior. At this particular men's event, we could almost see God's "Glory Cloud" descend as men ran to the altar to throw their lives to God with abandon, deeply repenting for anything unclean. Like that day I recounted in Boston, men began to throw on the stage whatever they considered to be a proof of their former lives, now abandoned in favor of a new life in Christ. It was powerful, emotionally draining, spiritually edifying, physically sanctifying, mentally illuminating and glorifying to God.

Vietnam veterans' hearts and minds that had suffered nightmares, bitterness, enmity and hatred were cleansed by the Word and the Spirit of Jesus Christ. Former adulterers declared their purification from lustful thoughts and desires. Husbands declared new love for wives, moved to be the men God created them to be and the husbands their wives desired them to be. What a glorious few hours we had!

God was so pleased with the repentance, faith, honesty, openness, truthfulness and reality the men were exhibiting that He freely poured out blessing upon blessing. Men experienced the primitive power of God working deep within them. One after another they stood to tell what God had done.

Pleasing God brought His favor, blessing, power and joy.

People spend hundreds, thousands, millions of dollars on drugs and alcohol to get Satan's counterfeit of the uninhibited joy and celebration of being a man. Doctors, lawyers and psychologists are, at this very moment, receiving monies from people who hope to obtain what God so freely gives.

To walk in God's will for our lives, as real men, secure in our manhood and our relationship with Him, is our highest good. Our highest good gives God pleasure.

Christians who contemplate how man displeases God often become blind to the Scriptures that describe how well we please Him. I read a letter from a minister last week about how God was going to judge the world in the "last days." There is a place for that, but the negative must not outweigh the positive message that men can give God pleasure!

At times, I don't please God. At times, I don't even please myself, and especially not others. But I press on, and on and on, knowing that, with increasing obedience, more often He is pleased than displeased.

The Bible counsels us to "have a walk worthy of the Lord, fully pleasing Him."[2] God accomplishes the "good pleasure of His will"[3] in us. "God works in you both to will and to do for His good pleasure."[4] *God does the work* in *us so He can be pleased* with *us.*

To walk in God's will for our lives, as real men, secure in our manhood and our relationship with Him, is our highest good. Our highest good gives God pleasure.

When we please God, we are working for our own highest good.

Jesus said, "Do not fear, little flock, for it is your Father's good pleasure to give you the kingdom."[5]

God works both to give and produce the Kingdom of God in us. That is where His pleasure is. God has no pleasure in wickedness,[6] nor the death of the wicked,[7] nor in fools, nor in the flesh, nor with those without faith in Him.[8]

Jesus said, "I do always those things that please Him."[9] Jesus had the testimony that He pleased God. God the Father even told the world, "This is My beloved Son, in whom I am well pleased."[10]

God was not just pleased in Jesus as deity, but God was pleased in the manhood that Jesus Christ displayed. We, like Jesus, give God pleasure when we—

- have faith in His Son[11]
- obey Him[12]
- are led by His Spirit[13]
- praise Him[14]

- serve Him[15]
- give to His ministry[16]

God takes pleasure in those who fear Him. God has pleasure in His people.[17] He is pleased when we risk looking foolish to share His Gospel with others so they can be saved.[18]

Even when we sin and bring guilt and condemnation in our life, it is possible to please God by our repentance.[19]

Pleasing God has the greatest benefit in the world (Heaven), gives the greatest satisfaction in life (reality) and achieves the greatest accomplishment in life (Christlikeness).

Whatever you have done or tried to be in life, however you have succeeded or failed, to what degree of manhood you have attained or come short, now is the time to make a quality decision to become a "real man."

Is Jesus real to you?

This is the place, you are the man, Christ is the Lord, and this is the time to pray this prayer with me. Mean it, and allow the Holy Spirit to begin a new work in your life at this moment.

Dear God, I am a man. I want to be a real man. So those things in my life that are wrong, where I have made mistakes, committed errors and sins, forgive me. I want them out of my life. Right now I ask you to come into my life by Your Spirit and change me. Make me to be the man You created me to be through Jesus Christ. Thank You, Lord. Amen.

Thank God you're a man.
Thank God you're real.
Be a real man!

Notes

Chapter 1
The Masculinity Crisis

1 David Nyhan, "Wanted: Some Stouthearted Men," *Boston Sunday Globe,* 7 May 1988, 87.
2 Jim Felton, "Soviets Can't Forget Horrors of World War II," *Daily Pilot,* 20 Sept. 1989, 12.
3 Proverbs 23:7 AMP
4 Edwin Louis Cole, *The Potential Principle* (Pittsburgh: Whitaker House, 1984), 72.
5 Judges 9:7-15
6 Genesis 13; 19

Chapter 2
The Substitute Society

1 Bill Murray, V*alues Clarification and the Christian* (Dallas: MFM Publishing, 1983), citing Richard A. Baer, "Parents, Schools, and Values Clarification," *Wall Street Journal,* 12 April 1982, 22.
2 Nicols Fox, "What Are Our Real Values?" *Newsweek,* 13 Feb. 1989, 8.
3 William Murchison, "Protestant Ethic Is Needed," *Dallas Morning News,* 23 Sept. 1989.
4 "Young Britain: A Survey of Youth Culture in Transition" by Euromonitor and Carrick James Market Research, London, 1987-1988.
5 Isaiah 5:20; Proverbs 17:15; Psalm 52:1
6 Romans 1:21-24; 8:29
7 Tim Robertson, *Pat Robertson's Perspective* (Virginia Beach, VA: CBN, 1987).
8 Paul Johnson, *Intellectuals* (New York: Harper and Row, 1988), 64-65.
9 Ibid, 23.

10 Mortimer B. Zuckerman, "Old Liberalism, New Politics," *U.S. News & World Report,* 7 Nov. 1988, 99.
11 Luke 7:33-34
12 John 15:13
13 2 Corinthians 7:9-11
14 Matthew 15:1-11
15 John 14:15
16 2 Timothy 4:3-4
17 Ezekiel 33:32 TLB
18 Matthew 19:16-22
19 Ezekiel 33:31 TLB
20 Ezekiel 33:32, James 1:22
21 Matthew 7:21
22 2 Chronicles 12:9-12
23 Jeremiah 24:7 AMP

Chapter 3
Cracks in the Mirror

1 Thomas C. Reeves, *A Question of Character* (Glencoe: Free Press, 1991).
2 Lee Colodny and Robert Gettlin, Silent Coup (New York: St. Martin's Press, 1991).
3 Joshua 4:14
4 1 Corinthians 5:11
5 1 Kings 12
6 Proverbs 20:29 TLB
7 2 Peter 2:19
8 Revelation 13
9 Proverbs 4:23
10 John 1:1
11 Hebrews 1:3; Colossians 1:15
12 Exodus 20:7
13 Genesis 25; Hebrews 12:16

Chapter 4
Behold the Man

1 Philippians 2:8 NIV
2 John 19:5
3 John 19:6
4 Matthew 27:24
5 John 19:19-20
6 John 1:4
7 Matthew 21:12
8 Matthew 23:13-33
9 John 8:7
10 John 8:11
11 Luke 4:24

12 Luke 4:30
13 John 19:26-27
14 Luke 6:12-13
15 Luke 22:39-46
16 Matthew 19:24
17 Matthew 16:23
18 Matthew 25:40
19 Matthew 25:31-46
20 John 13:1-17
21 John 13:8
22 Matthew 20:26-28
23 Mark 1:44
24 John 6:15
25 John 7:6
26 Romans 1:16
27 Philippians 2:10-11

Chapter 5
The Power of Life

1 Matthew 12:25
2 Psalm 86:11
3 1 Corinthians 3:22 TLB
4 1 Corinthians 15:53-54
5 Matthew 4:1-11
6 Romans 4:25
7 Matthew 10:39
8 2 Peter 1:4 AMP
9 Leviticus 25:8-55
10 1 Kings 18-19
11 1 Kings 19:4
12 Edwin Louis Cole, *When Life Is Just Too Tough* (Tulsa: Harrison House, 1988).
13 Romans 7:19
14 Romans 8:2
15 Philippians 3:13-14
16 Luke 22:41-44
17 James 2:18
18 John 10:10

Chapter 6
Life-Changing Values

1 John O. Anderson, *Cry of the Innocents* (South Plainfield NJ: Bridge Publishing, Inc., 1984), 41.
2 John O. Anderson, "Give Us Fathers," *CRY Ministry Newsletter,* 17 Aug. 1991, excerpt of Anderson's unpublished book, *Cry of Compassion.*

3 Michael Hirsley, "Giving Attitudes Are Giving Way," *Chicago Tribune,* 12 Oct. 1990, sec. 2, 8.
4 David Barton, America: *To Pray or Not to Pray* (Aledo, TX: Wall Builder Press, 1991), 10, 41, 68, 75.
5 2 Timothy 4:10
6 Genesis 25:29-34
7 Hebrews 11:26
8 Daniel 6
9 2 Chronicles 16:9 AMP
10 Daniel 3
11 Matthew 14:3-11
12 2 Corinthians 4:18
13 Proverbs 22:1
14 2 Peter 2:3
15 Jeremiah 23:25
16 John 10:11
17 1 Timothy 5:17
18 Luke 12:34
19 1 Corinthians 5:6; Galatians 5:9
20 1 Corinthians 5:11
21 2 Timothy 4:10
22 2 Peter 2:22
23 1 John 5:10

Chapter 7
Maximizing Your Resources

1 "Besieged Dinka Emphasize Physical, Social Stature," *Dallas Morning News,* 11 Sept. 1989.
2 Genesis 2:15
3 David D. Gilmore, "Manhood," *Natural History,* June 1990, 6-10.
4 David D. Gilmore as quoted by Russel Segal in "It's a World's Man," *Men's Health,* Dec. 1990, 46.
5 David D. Gilmore, *Masculinity in the Making: Cultural Concepts of Masculinity* (New Haven, CT: Yale University Press, 1990).
6 1 Peter 4:10
7 Genesis 1:26
8 John 17:12
9 Luke 12:48
10 1 Corinthians 4:2
11 Ecclesiastes 4:13
12 Genesis 26:15-33

13 *World Almanac* 1991 (New York: Scripps Howard Co., 1991), 467.
14 Ephesians 5:28-29
15 1 Timothy 3:1-12

Chapter 8
Staying on Top

1 Matthew 4:4; Deuteronomy 8:3
2 Matthew 3:17, 17:5; Acts 9:3-5
3 Judges 6:12; Matthew 1:20
4 Genesis 37:5; Matthew 1:20
5 Acts 10:10, 26:19; Revelation 1:9-20
6 Luke 2:26; Acts 13:2; Romans 8:14-16.
7 Luke 1:67-70; Ephesians 2:19-22; Hebrews 1:1
8 Acts 5:34; Proverbs 11:14
9 Psalm 37:4; 2 Peter 1:4; 2 Corinthians 5:17; Genesis 37
10 Psalm 107:20
11 John 1:1, 14; Malachi 4:2
12 Genesis 1:1-3; John 1:1
13 Habakkuk 2:4; Romans 1:17
14 1 Thessalonians 5:23
15 2 Corinthians 6:17
16 Acts 1:8
17 Romans 12:2
18 1 Thessalonians 2:13
19 Genesis 1:1
20 Matthew 9:17
21 Joshua 4:4-9
22 Judges 2:10
23 George Gallup, Jr., "Commentary on the State of Religion in the U.S. Today," *Gallup Poll,* 1984.
24 Exodus 16:16-21
25 Leonard LeSourd, *Strong Men/Weak Men* (Old Tappan, NJ: Chosen Books, 1990), 159.
26 John 15:5
27 Joshua 6-7
28 Genesis 3:6
29 Luke 22:45
30 1 Corinthians 2:9-10

Chapter 9
The Cornerstone of Character

1 2 Timothy 2:2
2 Deuteronomy 7:9
3 Hebrew 3:2
4 Luke 16:10 AMP
5 Matthew 25:14-30; Luke 19:12-27
6 Matthew 25:28-29
7 Matthew 25:24-26
8 Luke 16:12
9 James 1:22
10 2 Kings 3:11
11 Numbers 27:18
12 Hebrews 3:1-2
13 Proverbs 11:13
14 Galatians 5:19-21
15 Colossians 3:5
16 Ephesians 2:1-5
17 James 4:7
18 Ephesians 5:21
19 2 Samuel 15:1-6, 18:9-15
20 Luke 15:11-32
21 Ezekiel 33:30-33
22 Jeremiah 38:15

Chapter 10
Nothing but the Truth

1 John 14:6
2 John 8:32
3 2 Corinthians 4:4
4 "Lying, Cheating, Stealing: Ethics in Modern America," *ABC News,* 1 June 1989.
5 Garry Abrams, "Did We Rear A Bunch of 'Moral Mutants'?" *Los Angeles Times,* 11 Oct. 1990, E1, 7-8.
6 Isaiah 59:14
7 Jim Wright, "What Has Become of Trust?" *Dallas Morning News,* 26 Sept. 1989.
8 Leviticus 19:19
9 1 Timothy 5:22
10 John 8:44
11 Job 12:11 TLB
12 2 Samuel 11-12
13 2 Samuel 12:7
14 2 Samuel 12; Psalm 51
15 1 Samuel 13:5-14
16 1 Samuel 13:14
17 Luke 12:2 NIV
18 Numbers 32:23
19 James C. Dobson, *Love Must Be Tough* (Waco, TX: Word Books, 1983), 44.

20 Matthew 5:23-24
21 John 8:32
22 Proverbs 23:23

Chapter 11
Love or Lust
1 John 3:16
2 Hebrews 11:25
3 Genesis 19:4-5
4 Marco R. della Cava,
"Sexual Addiction Can
Lead to Destruction,"
USA Today, 2 Feb.
1989, 5D.
5 Luke 4:34
6 Matthew 8:29
7 Proverbs 29:27
8 1 John 2:16
9 Genesis 3:6
10 John 17:3
11 Matthew 6:22;
Luke 11:34
12 Titus 1:15
13 James Dobson, *Focus
on the Family,*
March 1990.
14 David Jackson,
"Minister Pleads Guilty
to Rapes," *Dallas
Morning News,* 25 Aug.
1989, 33A, 36A.
15 U.S. Department of
Justice, Office of
Juvenile Justice and
Delinquency Prevention,
Principal Investigator
Judith A. Reisman,
Ph.D., "Executive
Summary: Images of
Children, Crime and
Violence in Playboy,
Penthouse and Hustler
Magazines,"
Nov. 1987.
16 "Peep Shows Incite
Man to Rape,"
*Christian Voice
Washington Report,*
July 1984.
17 Genesis 6:5
18 Genesis 19:24-29
19 U.S. Department, Office
of Juvenile Justice and
Delinquency Prevention,
Principal Investigator
Judith A. Resiman,
Ph.D., "Executive
Summary: Images of
Children, Crime and
Violence in Playboy,
Penthouse and Hustler
Magazines, "
Nov. 1987, 3.

20 George Flesh, "Why I
Quit Doing Abortions,"
Los Angeles Times,
12 Sept. 1991, B11.
21 George Grant, *Grand
Illusions: The Legacy of
Planned Parenthood*
(Brentwood, TN:
Wolgemuth and Hyatt
Publishers, Inc.,
1988), 61.
22 John 8:44
23 John 8:49
24 Romans 1:26-32
25 Galatians 5:16
26 Ephesians 4:22-23
27 Romans 8:37
28 James 1:2
29 Job 31:1
30 Titus 2:11-12 NIV

Chapter 12
Royal Pursuits
1 John 3:3
2 Matthew 6:33
3 Colossians 3:23
4 2 Thessalonians 3:10
5 Zechariah 4:10
6 Luke 13:9, my own
paraphrase
7 Proverbs 16:7
8 1 John 2:27
9 John 15:7
10 1 Samuel 16:7
11 Genesis 13:4
12 Joshua 1:8
13 Matthew 6:33

Chapter 13
The Cost of Greatness
1 Matthew 20:26-27
2 John 13:1-17
3 Matthew 20:28
4 Hebrews 1:14
5 Luke 9:48 TLB
6 2 Peter 1:5-7
7 Genesis 3
8 Genesis 3:12
9 Revelation 12:10
10 1 Samuel 13:11
11 2 Samuel 12:16-17
12 1 Samuel 30:1-19
13 1 Timothy 1:13,15
14 1 Corinthians 11:1 NIV
15 Romans 12:19
16 Matthew 20:26

Chapter 14
The Winning Strategy
1 Proverbs 4:7
2 James 1:5
3 1 Kings 3:4-14

4 James 3:15
5 James 3:17
6 Proverbs 3:16-17
7 Psalm 111:10
8 1 Kings 3:6-7
9 Isaiah 11:2
10 1 Corinthians 1:30
11 James 1:5
12 Ephesians 3:10
13 Proverbs 1:29-31
14 Proverbs 1:7; 23:9
15 Luke 16:1-8
16 Ezekiel 28:14-17
17 2 Kings 5:11 TLB
18 2 Kings 5:13 TLB
19 Proverbs 19:3 TLB
20 1 Corinthians 1:31
21 2 Corinthians 3:18
22 Edwin Louis Cole, *The
Potential Principle*
(Pittsburgh: Whitaker
House, 1984), 14.
23 Proverbs 8:11
24 Proverbs 2:4-6

Chapter 15
Employed for Life
1 Morris Cerullo, *Proof
Producers* (San Diego:
Morris Cerullo World
Evangelism, 1979), 25.
2 2 Thessalonians 3:10
3 John 10:10
4 2 Timothy 4:5
5 1 Corinthians 15:58

Chapter 16
Financial Freedom
1 Exodus 35
2 Malachi 1:6
3 Luke 18:9-14
4 Matthew 26:8-9
5 John 12:4-6
6 Matthew 26:11
7 Psalm 50:12-15
8 Luke 6:38
9 1 Timothy 6:6
10 Matthew 6:21
11 Exodus 34:26
12 Proverbs 3:9
13 Malachi 3:8
14 Leviticus 27:30
15 Malachi 3:11
16 Luke 6:38
17 2 Corinthians 8:1-5
18 Luke 19:5-9
19 Acts 10:2-8
20 2 Corinthians 8
21 Luke 16:9
22 Mark 11:12-14
23 1 Samuel 15:22
24 John 14:21

25 Edwin Louis Cole, *The Potential Principle* (Pittsburgh: Whitaker House, 1984).

26 Matthew 26:13

Chapter 17
Postive Stress

1 "Research Recommendations," issued by National Institute of Business Management, 6 March 1989, 2.

2 Ian Ball, "Now They Say TV Isn't Even Relaxing," *The [London] Times,* July 1990, citing Dr. Robert Kubey and Dr. Mihaly Csikszentminhalyi, *Television and the Quality of Life: How Viewing Shapes Everyday Experience* (Hillsdale, NJ: Erlbaum, Lawrence, and Associates, Inc., 1990).

3 Ian Ball, "Now They Say TV Isn't Even Relaxing," citing David Frost.

4 Fred Williams, "Office Stress Follows Many Home," *USA Today,* 15 March 1990, 8B, citing survey by Dunhill Personnel System, Inc.

5 "Study Finds a Paying Job Helps Women Beat the Blues," *Orange County Register,* 5 Sept. 1990, K2, citing study by R. Jay Turner, sociology professor at University of Toronto.

6 Dr. T. Berry Brazelton, "Working Parents," *Newsweek,* 13 Feb. 1989, 66-70.

7 Proverbs 24:10 TLB

8 John 5:19-20

9 John 10:30-42

10 John 14:12, 10:37-38

11 Matthew 7:29

12 James 1:2-4

13 Romans 5:3-5

14 1 Peter 1:6-7

15 Revelation 3:12

16 Philippians 4:6

17 1 Peter 5:9

18 James 1:12; Romans 8:35-37

19 1 Peter 4:12-13

20 Genesis 50:20

Chapter 18
Peace for All Seasons

1 Marlin Maddoux, *The Selling of Gorbachev* (Dallas: International Christian Media, 1988), 65-66.

2 James Reston, "Down Below the Summits, Millions of War Deaths," *The New York Times,* 3 June 1988, I-31.

3 2 Samuel 15

4 2 Samuel 15:2

5 2 Samuel 17:23

6 Psalm 55:12-14

7 Psalm 55:21

8 Luke 2:14 AMP

9 Luke 4

10 John 14:27

11 Galatians 5:17

12 James 4:1

13 Romans 8:6

14 Romans 6:16

15 Matthew 11:30

16 Matthew 18:8-9

17 Proverbs 25:26

18 Joshua 9

19 Luke 11:17

20 Psalm 86:11

21 Romans 14:19

22 1 Corinthians 6:12

23 Romans 6:16

24 Genesis 16, 18

25 Genesis 16:11-12.

26 Hebrews 4:9

27 1 Timothy 6:6

28 Luke 17:21

29 John 14:27; Philippians 4:7; Psalm 119:165

30 1 Corinthians 14:33

31 Isaiah 9:6

32 John 14:27

33 Colossians 3:15 AMP

34 Ephesians 2:14-17

35 Acts 15

36 Matthew 26:63

37 Luke 19:42 AMP

Chapter 19
Leadership That Works

1 John 10:30

2 John 5:30, 6:38

3 Mark 11:15-17

4 1 Timothy 3

5 Proverbs 22:1

6 Mike McKinley, "Secretary of the Navy Challenges Navy's Leaders," *All Hands,* Feb. 1988, 14-15.

7 2 Chronicles 15:16-17

8 Ephesians 5:26

9 Esther 4:14

10 Habakkuk 2:3

Chapter 20
The Irresistible Husband

1 Galatians 5:22-23 NIV

2 Galatians 5:19-21

3 Philippians 2:3

4 2 Samuel 22:36

5 Romans 12:10

6 Ephesians 4:2; Colossians 3:12

7 Numbers 12:3

8 Kay Ray, "In Houston, Women Lead," *USA Today,* 2 July 1990, 2.

9 Jan Halper, "Male Mystique," *American Way Magazine,* 1 August 1989, 42-48.

Chapter 21
The Fabulous Father

1 Australia Children's Television Foundation.

2 William Raspberry, "Kids Need a Moral Compass to Go Straight," *Los Angeles Times,* 26 Oct. 1990.

3 Judge Moore, Los Angeles, CA. Personal quotation. Reprinted by permission.

4 Ibid.

5 Michael Oreskes, "U.S. Youth in the '90s: The Indifferent Generation," *Washington Post,* citing The Times Mirror Center for the People and Press Report and People for the American Way, *New York Times,* 28 June 1990, A1.

6 Ibid.

7 Bob Larson, Larson's *Book of Cults* (Wheaton, IL: Tyndale House Publishers, 1982), 32.

8 Ibid.

9 1 Kings 1:6 TLB

10 Ephesians 6:4

11 3 John 4

Chapter 22
The Authentic Friend

1 Victor Ostrovsky and Claire Hoy, *By Way of Deception: Making and Unmaking of a Mossad Officer* (New York: St. Marton's Press, 1990), 86.
2 Ibid, 98.
3 2 Samuel 13
4 Psalm 41:9
5 Luke 23:34
6 Galatians 4:9
7 Hebrews 10:35
8 John 16:33
9 1 Peter 1:7
10 Proverbs 18:24
11 John 15:15
12 Proverbs 27:6
13 Proverbs 17:17
14 John 15:13
15 2 Samuel 15:30-37
16 2 Samuel 16-17
17 Job 2:9
18 Proverbs 18:24
19 2 Samuel 1:26
20 James 2:23
21 Exodus 33:11

Chapter 23
The Greatest Pleasure in Life

1 Charles Handy, "Thought for the Day," London, 17 Dec. 1986.
2 Colossians 1:10
3 Ephesians 1:5
4 Philippians 2:13
5 Luke 12:32
6 Psalm 5:4
7 Ezekiel 18:23, 33:11
8 Romans 8:8; Hebrews 11:6
9 John 8:29
10 Matthew 3:17
11 Hebrews 11:6
12 1 John 3:22
13 Romans 8:14
14 Psalm 69:30-31
15 John 12:26
16 2 Corinthians 9:7
17 Psalm 149:4
18 1 Corinthians 1:21
19 Psalm 51:19

NANCY CORBETT COLE CHARITIES

 A portion of the proceeds from this book will be given to Nancy Corbett Cole Charities, serving the abused, addicted and abandoned. Internationally, "Nancy Corbett Cole Homes of Refuge" provide housing, vocational training and education for abused women and children. In the United States, help is ongoing on an individual and corporate basis.

Nancy Corbett Cole, "The Loveliest Lady in the Land," supported her husband, Edwin Louis Cole, for 54 years in pursuing his life's mission. Behind the scenes, she was a spiritual anchor and provider for many. Before her death in December 2000, Nancy asked for the assurance that those for whom she had provided would not feel her absence. To fulfill that end, and for that purpose, Nancy Corbett Cole Charities were established.

By purchasing this book, you have helped society's under-served and less privileged members. If this book helped you, please consider sending a generous donation as well. Your one-time or continual support will help the helpless, heal the hurting and relieve the needy. Your gift is fully tax-deductible in the U.S. Send your compassionate contribution to:

Nancy Corbett Cole Charities
P. O. Box 92501
Southlake, TX 76092
USA
Thank you for your cheerful and unselfish care for others.

Watch for More Watercolor Books®

by terrific authors like –

Edwin Louis Cole	Donald Ostrom
Nancy Corbett Cole	Steve Riggle
Karen Davis	G. F. Watkins
Ron DePriest	Many more!

watercolor books®

Southlake, Texas

www.watercolorbooks.com

ABOUT THE AUTHOR

Edwin Louis Cole, an internationally-acclaimed speaker, best-selling author and motivational lecturer, was known for his practical application of wisdom from kingdom principles. Through his books, tapes and videos, the ministry to men continues to reach thousands of men worldwide, challenging them to fulfill their potential for true manhood, which is Christlikeness. His books have sold in the millions, including the landmark *Maximized Manhood*. Over five million people have studied his principles in the last fifty years. Considered "the father of the Christian men's movement," Edwin Louis Cole commissioned other men who now travel extensively worldwide to strengthen the ministry he founded under the divine guidance of the Holy Spirit.

Dr. Cole's lifetime body of work is being compiled at
www.EdColeLibrary.com

For more information, write:
Ed Cole Library
P.O. Box 92921
Southlake, TX 76092

Also by Edwin Louis Cole

Revised Version Maximized Manhood
The Power of Potential
Strong Men in Tough Times
ManPower
Absolute Answers to Prodigal Problems
COURAGE
Winners Are Not Those Who Never Fail but
Those Who NEVER QUIT!
Communication, Sex and Money
The Unique Woman
TREASURE
Manhood 101
Profiles in Courageous Manhood
Irresistible Husband
Sexual Integrity

Study curriculum available for most books.

www.watercolorbooks.com